*From Len to Lil
With Love and a Lick.*

Copyright © Ashley Burgoyne 2020

ashleyburgoyne.wixsite.com/writerandcomposer

First Edition published in 2020

ISBN: 9798612668466

The right of Ashley Burgoyne to be identified as the Author of this work has been asserted by them in accordance with the Copyright, Designs and Patents Act 1988.

All rights reserved. No part of this publication may be reproduced, stored in a retrieval system, or transmitted in any form or by any means, electronic, mechanical, photocopying, recording or otherwise, without the prior permission of the author.

No one shall upload this title, or part of this title, to any social media websites.

Foreword by Mike Doyle

My Father, Basil Leonard Doyle, or 'Len' as he was known to everybody (he apparently dropped 'Basil' at an early age!) died on 15th August 2005, aged 84. He outlived my mother, Lilian Rose Doyle (known as 'Lily', or 'Lil' to family and close friends), by ten years. Lily died on 31st August 1995 at age 75.

When I was sorting through Dad's possessions after his death, I came across an old Terry's chocolate box, tied with a red ribbon. Upon opening it, I found a trove of letters. I had never seen them before. The letters had been written by Dad to Mum when they were courting.

The first letters were undated. After 21st June 1939, most were dated. The penultimate letter was dated 16th August 1944, when Lil and Len were making their wedding arrangements. They were to marry on 10th September 1944. After that, there were no more letters for five years, until one final letter, which was dated 27th May 1949 – the day I was born.

I was mesmerised by them. They made me laugh, and they made me cry, and they filled me with a tremendous longing to be able to see Mum and Dad together for one last time.

I was subsequently unable to trace any letters in the other direction, from my mum to my dad. What became of them? I don't know, but I assume that it was my mum who had kept all of Dad's letters, put them in that Terry's chocolate box, and tied a red ribbon around them.

I soon came to realise that those letters were not only a document of Mum and Dad's courtship (albeit from one side only!), but an unfolding story of two young lovers living and courting in London through World War II. This was a historic archive. The Battle of Britain, the London Blitz, and much more, are there – all being described in a quite matter-of-fact way, as Lily and Len went about their daily lives.

Lily and Len's courtship spanned London. Mum lived in relatively affluent Neasden in North West London. Dad was an East End boy, living in Bow, above a pawnbroker's shop. Although most of the letters have a jovial tone, Len was living near the docks on the Thames, which were a regular target for Nazi bombs during the Blitz. Some of his descriptions of cataclysmic events as a routine occurrence are sobering. True 'Blitz Spirit'!

At this point I must express huge gratitude to my daughter Jenny and her husband Ashley. I told Jenny of discovering Len's letters, and she took it upon herself to collate them and organise them into a timeline (something of a challenge, as several letters were undated). Ashley then came forward with the idea of publishing them. The result is the publication you are reading now.

Jenny, Ashley and I feel it's appropriate that this book is published in 2020 – the centenary of Lily's birth.
It's also the 99th anniversary of Len's birth, and the 76th anniversary of their wedding.

Why 'With Love and a Lick'?
Read on and find out …

Michael John Doyle
Proud son of Basil Leonard Doyle and Lilian Rose Doyle

For my children – Jenny, John, Matthew and Hannah
In memory of Nanna and Grandad

March 2020

Introduction by Ashley Burgoyne

I first met Len in 1998. My 'wife-to-be' took me down to the south coast where I was introduced to this wonderful, colourful character with a great sense of humour.

He often talked of his work at The Plessey Company, which he joined in 1943 and stayed with until his retirement in the 1980s. Although he often talked of his late wife, Lily, he never mentioned their correspondence during the war – why would he!? I was, therefore, as surprised as the rest of the family to hear of the box of letters which Lily, and then Len, had kept safe for all those years.

My wife, Jenny, painstakingly ordered and typed up these letters back in 2005/06 so immediate family could read them. Then, having written and published a few books, I came across the typed-up letters and felt that publishing the letters would be the most perfect way of remembering Len and Lily. Not just for family and friends, but also for historians; as they do give the reader a real sense of what it was like to live in London during World War II.

During my research, photos were unearthed, which have been included (apologies for the quality – they're old!) and with the help of Mike, and Len and Lily's niece Pat in Australia, some names have been put to faces in the photos.

I would like to end my introduction by sharing a short story about Len. When he was in his early 80s, my wife and I took him out to a local eatery. The meal was extremely poor (and the name of the eatery will, therefore, remain nameless!) Len's hearing wasn't great. His hearing aids would often squeal away and Len would raise his voice several decibels above the norm! Having eaten most of the main course, Len declared how bad it was in what can only be described as a loud voice! Whilst we were trying to get him to lower his voice, a waitress came over and said that she'd heard him, and the drinks would be on the house. Len immediately ordered another drink! Dessert was consumed and Len, once more, made it clear that it was bad. The waitress was upon us in a flash, beckoning us to leave and informing us that the whole meal was on the house. "If that's the case," said Len, "I'll have seconds!" With the waitress's eyes burning holes in the back of our heads, we ushered Len to the exit!

From the following letters I think you'll find that his sense of humour, and mischievousness, remained with Len from 1939 until 2005!

    Enjoy,

        Ashley

    PS To keep these letters as authentic as possible, they are transcribed exactly as they are written – including all spelling errors.

1939

(*Undated letter 1*)

Read this outside paper first

Enclosed is the essence of my conversation with Francis yesterday.
 I have recorded some of my thoughts, in brackets. The reason I have written the conversation down – although I have condensed it to as few as words as possible – is because it would be impossible for me to tell it to you without treating it as a joke – which it is not. I sincerely assure you that I have added nothing from my own imagination (which is a vivid one) to the paper.
 Glover has rumbled, and bumped it out of me last night.
 yours,
 young and inexperienced.

 P.S. – what ab'aht

D=Doyle   F=Francis   L=the unknown girl

1
Here is a brief summary of my conversation with F :-

F:- "ar'nt you taking Lil out any more, D?"

D:- "I may do so, but do not know if she would like to come"

F:- "Of course she would like to go with you, but she's as shy and backward as you are. You both want to go out together, yet each is too shy to ask the other"

D (Blustering to gain time):- But if I ask L, and she agrees, how do I know that she really wants to come with a little 'erb like me? She may say "yes" just because she's a good sort, and would not like to "let me down"

F:- "Don't be silly! She likes you ever such a lot; and you like her as well, don't you?"

D (Blushing furiously):- "Not 'arf"

F:- "Well, why don't you take her to the "flicks" * or visit her and have tea with her one Sunday?

D (Wishing earth would open and swallow him) :- "Dunno. Just too shy to ask, I suppose. If she really wanted me to do so, I expect she would drop a hint"

F "You know L is more backward than you are, in coming forward. Why not arrange to go out with her regularly? Your the only boy friend she has.

D (almost crying with remorse):- "I'll see what I can do" (then, struck with good excuse and bright idea):- "But I can't afford it regularly".

F:- "Gam! she's not a dear girl to take out"

D:- "I would'nt take her out if she were not. I like a cuddle now and again (Then D, suddenly realising he had put his foot in it) "Oh! You mean dear in the money sense! I thought you meant the other 'dear' (similar to darling)"

F:- "Well, you will ask her, won't you?"

D (seeing escape at last) "yes! Not 'arf."

   The conversation was ended by D's print being mashed up in washer, thus bringing forth curses from D.

"flicks" – pictures (or cinema)

*

4

(Undated letter 2)

O.K. for Sat. I will call for you straight from work. I may have to work 'till 1.0 p.m.

I will wear my best clothes under my overalls, to save carrying them. We will probably return early (VERY early) Mon morn., so let your mother know.

Try and buy ½ lb box of good chocs (Terrys if possible) for us to eat on train.

I very much like the "Hat" you wore Last Sun.

Hoping things at Home are improving,

Len

P.S. – No reply. Taken for granted.

*

(Undated letter 3)

On Whit Monday or Tuesday, I intend to visit the Science Museum and Natural History Museums after having a boat out on the Serpentine, Hyde Park.

I wondered if you would care to accompany me, as nobody else will come (I have not asked anybody yet, and if you come do not intend to do so). As I know you will say yes, I suggest that we should go early in the afternoon, and the best plan would be for me to meet you at Baker Street Station, as all the trains from Neasden stop at Baker Street.

The time we can arrange later.

When we went to Hendon, I had a most enjoyable time, but owing to M, Monday was rather a disconcerting (good word, what? – Where's that dictionary!) and embarising (one r or two?) day for us both.

It is for this reason that I am expressing myself in writing, instead of using the gift of the gab.

Hoping everything will be O.K (real hopes, or some hopes?), yours sincerely

Basil LENARD (please note) Doyle

P.S. Somebody is at the bottom of this, but taint me.

N.B – Not a bean.

*

(Undated letter 4)

I have, this week, taken a special course in lifesaving at the Poplar Baths. I will also bring along two lifebelts, one raft, distress signals, two firearms (in case we are marooned on a savage island), and provisions to last for three months.

yours sincerely
B.L.D.*

P.S. Please excuse me for boring you with such a long letter. I have been so fed up this week, in having no company but my own during the evenings, and only housework to do, that at last I decided to go in for a spot of writing. The result you have seen, as above.

* B.L.D. is an abbreviation for either one of the following:-

    (i)   Brilliant, Latitudinarium (look it up in a dictionary) & Delightful

    (ii)   Balmy, Lackadaisical & Daft

    (iii)   Basil, Lenard Doyle.

Now – WHAT DO YOU THINK?

*

(Undated letter 5)

I would beg to suggest the following plan:-
    1. You reach Neasden station at 1.30. assuming you get a fairly early train, you should be at Baker Street by 2.0. Fast trains leave platform 4: slow train, platform 3. (you will probably have to have the slow train).
    2. I will meet you on the platform at Baker Street – DO NOT LEAVE THE PLATFORM WHERE YOUR TRAIN COMES IN.
    3. The cheapest way will be to get a return ticket to Baker Street, which will cost about 1/- (single 8d or 9d).
    4. MONDAY, I think will be the best day, although we may have to wait some time for a boat. If I go out with Glover, it will probably be on Tuesday.

P.S. – the Science Museum is ~~lousy~~ lovely.

yours, Marmaduke Clarence Archibald

*

(Undated letter 6)

Next Saturday afternoon, 10 June, I intend to visit the stall picture-theatre, Kingsway, to see the film "Storm over Bengal", and if I have time afterwards may have a boat out in Hyde Park.
    Would you care to come? If so, meet me at Baker Street at 1.45 – 2.0 if this time is OK with you. If you do not wish to come, do not be <u>afraid to say so: I will in no way be offended</u>.
    No one aint behind this 'cept me. If we go on a boat you'll do the splashing – not me (I hope)
                      Yours sincerely
                            Lenard Doyle.

P.S. – Have just remembered you have night school exam on June 10. Make the date, therefore, June 17 – o.k.?
    I will be in the shops next week, and if I have dinner in the canteen, may not have time to enter the vault during the dinner-hour. If, therefore, you have any alterations, additions, modifications or rejections to make to the above plans, you know my address – 101/103 Burdett Rd, Bow, London E3. If I hear nothing from you, then I will assume that everything is O.K., and will turn up at Baker Street on June 17 at 1.45 (p.m.)

*

(Undated letter 7)

PRIVIT LETTER

What arrangements shall I make for the carnival?
 Although, on Saturday, I said I would love to come (and I mean that most sincerely), we omitted (is omitted spelt omitted or omitted? – or ommited?) anyhow, we forgot to make any detailed planifications – I know there aint no such werd, but it sound better than plans – and the following suggestions have entered my mind (my mind being almost empty, there is still plenty of room for any suggestions that you care to make).

    Shall I:-
- i. Meet you at some prearranged point, the aforesaid point being chosen by mutual agreement, at a prearranged time, ditto.
- ii. Call on you after I have had some grub in Neasden.
- iii. Wait at the works, and meet you near there.

As I can only write up to three in Roman numerals (so four iv or vi? – never can I remember), it is impossible for me to make any more suggestions.
 The reason I have delivered this letter as early as today is because I may not have time to visit the vault on Wednesday or ~~Thirsty~~ Thursday.

(above is all the shorthand I know)

<u>P.T.O</u>

yours sincerely

    Lenard Doyle

Copies to:-
Old Nick, the bottle – washer
The man in the moon
Old King Cole
Henry the Eighth
Neville Chamberlain
Miss L. Smith.

(attached)

Dear Lily,
    My holiday address is, as described by landlady;-
        Mr. B.L.Doyle,
          c/o Mrs P. Hopper,
            21 Milward Road,
              Hastings,
                East Sussex.

Bed and Breakfast. Terms moderate. Two minutes from sea.

Yours sincerely

    Lenard.

*

(First dated letter!)

21-6-39 written and
composed at
evening classes.

Dear Lily,

Many thanks for your letter, which I received at 1.31 ½ a.m. yesterday, the aforesaid being delivered by special messenger boy, whom I tipped 1 ½ d, 4 fag cards, 3 marbles and a picture of Madeline Carrol (both words spelt wrong – I know!) for his kind services.

To save either of us writing (especially if it's raining), I will call for you at 1.15 – 1.30.

Owing to unforeseen circumstances which have happened to my old Pot and Pan – the old man – that is, my father – today, it may be necessary to make our date for Sunday, July 1, one week earlier, that is, on June 25 (the day after the carnival). I thought I had better let know now, and I sincerely hope that this alteration has not "mucked you up" in any way and that you will be able to come with me on June 25, if your parents have no objection to us going out together two days running.

I will give a full explanation to you on Saturday.

I have sent a letter to that remarkable man, the Clerk of the Weather, asking him to let it be fine on Saturday; I hope he won't let us down.

Yours sincerely
Lenard Doyle.

P.T.O

Post Script. – If it rains we'll go to the flicks.

*

28.6.39. Evening Classes, Mathematics.

I will be staying to Mummy's and Daddy's Day, but if it ends by 6.30p.m, intend to visit the Granada, Willesden, to see Bryan Michies Discoveries, and, of course, the films (which include one of the Royal Tour !?!!*!!!*!!)
If I go, would you care to accompany me?
It will be very hard to decide beforehand whether I will be going or not, as I have no idea whatsoever what time the old jossers who make the speeches, finish gassing – what?
If you are staying at Parents day, we can go straight from the works.
If you are not staying, then the whole question boils down to this:- Will you be at home Saturday evening?
IF YOU ALREADY HAVE AN ENGAGEMENT, OR DO NOT WISH TO COME, PLEASE DO NOT BE AFRAID TO SAY SO.
If you will be at home on Saturday evening, may I call for you between 5.30 and 6.30? If I am not at your home by 6.45 or 7.0 (lots of "ifs" in this document aint there?), then I will not be coming at all, and hope you will not be disappointed.
As you see, it is very difficult to say whether I am going to the cinema or no, it depending upon whether Parents day ends early enough. Please, therefore, let me know on Friday if this is O.K?

P.T.O

yours sincerely

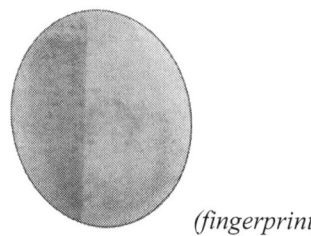
(fingerprint)

(Len Doyle)
(Scotland yard may have record of the above signature)

P.S – If you stay to serve on Saturday, I will give you some tummy-ache powder, to put in my sisters tea.
Just one more thing –
IF I get a medal, I will certainly go to the cinema, to celebrate.

N.B. – Please make sure to place powder in Sisters tea – NOT IN MINE.

*

101/103 Burdett Road,

Bow,

London E.3

6/7/39

Dear Lily,
	As it is your birthday on Sunday, I would like you to know that I have not forgotten it. I did intend to send you a gift through the post, but on second thoughts (proverbially the best), I decided to hold it over until you return, firstly because it might arrive at your house after you had left – which would be a catastrophe – and secondly , because it is edible, and if you were as greedy as I am (which you are certainly not), whacking it out with mother, father and two sisters (which you, being the girl you are, would probably do) would reduce its quantity by four-fifths. Please do not think I want your family to be left out; certainly not: it is just my nature to write like I do. You see, I never share anything with my sister, and seldom have anything to share with my parents. I thought you might be the same, but know you are not. And if this aint Irish, I'll eat my hat. (Good job I have no hat). Anyhow, the real truth of the matter is that I am too shy to send it to you openly.
	After careful thought, I decided to pass the time by writing a lyric, as per follows.

Original poem by Doyle (alias, Mr. Anon.)

1
Hoping that this arrives before you away,
I wish you many Happy Returns of the day,
May your holiday be hilarious,
Do not make it too gastronomerous,
Eat well, sleep well, do not work,
Don't do nuffink, but just shirk
All that which pertains to work.

2
I know this is some hours too early
To wish you a delightful birthday,
But on Sunday the G.P.O. refuses,
To deliver any form of news'es,
Even from old B.L.D,
    They simply take no notice of me,
But I'll get even with them one day,
I'll just phone up the I.R.A.
And ask them to blow the bally lot up,
Then I won't be such a blooming big mutt.

3
To return to your birthday,
Be sure to make it a great mirthday,
Think of my mug – I don't know why –
And you'll laugh until you cry,
But don't blame me, 'taint my fault,
I'm such an ugly looking gawk,
My mother and father are quite handsome,
So you can't blame them for this unfortunate accident.

4
Now, your present aint bin forgotten,
I promise you, it won't get rotten,
It is here, hearty and hale,
'tis impossible for it to get stale,
The present is such, it can be used only once,
I could obtain nothing else, being such a dunce,
It's a sweetmeat, you see, and I hope you'll enjoy it.
One day, when alone, to your mitts I'll convey it,
Which unfortunately won't be for two or three weeks,
By which time I'll have the jeeps.

This verse is getting far too long,
So I'll desist before I go wrong.

Wishing you Many Happy Returns, and that your mother, father, your sisters and yourself have a glorious holiday,
    Yours most sincerely,

Lenard

P.T.O.

P.S. I was going to write some more poem,
But could think of no words to rhyme with muddle and fuddled and lisped.
Perhaps you could help me?

*

(Undated letter 8)

Dear Lily,
    I know this is very early to let you know about the arrangements for Sunday, but I may not be entering the vault during the dinner hour for the rest of this week (yes, I know you've heard that one before, but this time I really mean it (?))
    The 'S' plan – er, sorry, that's the wrong one – the plan is as follows:-

1. I meet you at Baker Street station (NEWS THEATRE) not later than 9.15 a.m, and not earlier than 4.30 am. 'hem.
2. Thence we proceed to Waterloo.
3. From Waterloo we go to Leatherhead.
4. If I can remember the way (which I probably can't), we will go, by a devious route, to the Sussex Gliding Club's field (about 12(?) miles)
5. We will rest on the grass boundary of the club until 6.0p.m.
6. Another two miles crawl *(crossed out)* walk will bring us to a tea house, where, naturally, we'll have tea.
7. Half a mile form the tea house is the station, and thus we return to London.

I advise you to leave all high-heeled shoes at home.

    I will bring along two ~~sandw~~ bits of grub and four apples, just in case we get hungry.
    Listen to the weather forecast for Sunday on Saturday, and if it is excellent, don't bring your raincoat. If it is doubtful, then use your discretion.
    I assure you I will make the outing as enjoyable as possible, and I hope you will not get too tired.
    If I hear nothing from you, I will assume that everything is O.K. Please do not be afraid to write to me if you wish to make any additions, subtractions, alterations or modifications to these plans.

    I may bring a camera.

                    yours sincerely
                        Leonard.

P.S. – Do you remember the letter you received from me on Friday, 7 July, when I asked for words to ryme with fuddle, muddle and miss? Well, thanks for your help in the Granada, I have at least found words to go with muddle and miss.
   Oh, by the way, bring your sisters watch if possible.

*

(Post Card Dated 10th July 1939)

To Lily,
         Many thanks for your kind letter, whisk arrived thish morning. I hic! I hic! Reached Hashtingshs shafe shound yesterday, and am not lonely here, as I have already dishcovered an old school friend (boy). We've jus' bin celebrating. Re your last line, I promish to behave myself. Aforsaid' friend is woman – hater, sho, you shee, I'm in shafe handshs.
                      Cheerio!
                      Lenard.
P.S.- I hope you don't think I've been drinking.

*

(Post Card Dated 13th July 1939)

Dear Lily,
Edgar (that's name of pre-mentioned friend) and myself are having glorious time at Hastings, and he is keeping me well under control.
    It's always 'Eyes front' for me now, never 'Eyes right' or 'Eyes left' and certainly not 'Eyes down'.
    We are taking the following program today. Either:-
(i)   ~~Boose~~ Cruise to Eastbourne and airplane flight, or:-
(ii)   Cruise to Boulogne. We are at present having debate (?) on subject. When I've finished punching his head, I think we'll go to Eastbourne and flight.

Did you receive my postcard on Tuesday? I am not sure whether I put 'Kent' on the address. Hope you are having as good as time as we are,
        Yours sincerely,
        LEONARD.
I have just received your card.
Good old West Ham!

P.S – H-Hav-ve j-j-just b-b-bin ffor fuf-fuf-flight, I-It wus fuf-fine, I was'nt bi-bif-frightened.
For microscopic writing, apply Doyle & Edgar, Box 131, Etc.

*

(Real Photogravure Letter Card Dated 14th July 1939)

To Miss. L. Smith
c/o Mrs. S. Spratling
51, Thanet Road,
Margate,
Kent.

From THE MAN IN THE MOON
(BROTHER OF OLD NICK)

Dear Lily,
    The weather, up to and including Thursday has been excellent, but today (Friday) is not too good. Owing to this, Edgar and myself have decided to write, between us, a lot of bosh, and to post it to all our friends and relations. He is helping me to compose this, all blots, smudges and misspellings (three es'es?) are contributions from him; everything else by me.
    If you manage to finish reading this without being bored stiff, then you are a hero, and deserve the V.C.
Well, here goes:-
We went in a speedboat yesterday evening.
The dratted cover blew away, and we got soaked.
As we couldn't get much wetter, we went round again. Then the bloke who drives the boat said that if we stayed on, to encourage other people to take the trip, (we had had the boat to ourselves, so far) he would take us round for half price; this we did, and went round once more, with four middle-aged persons as fellow-passengers. We are just about to alight, when three young females got in.
    Edgar, the beast (who, up to now has always been a woman-hater), said 'lets go round again' and I feebly consented, and thanked the almighty that I had paid for my board and lodging, and had a return ticket to London.
    Well, these females also got drenched, and as they could'nt get much wetter, went round again. Edgar asked me to do likewise, and as I was in a state of collapse, and could not speak, he took that silence give consent, and once more, away we went. Well, these females alighted after their second trip, but not us. You see, the driver said

that as we had been such good customers, he would give us another trip for nothing if we waited 'till he got another six passengers. Thus, we had six trips straight off: total cost 9/- each. There was no supper for us that night, and I have been able to afford no solid food since. Edgar, I believe, now has a cold (which serves him right). He returns home tomorrow – thank goodness.

 Tripe, by Doyle:-
My Hastings holiday is over,
But I've another yet to come.
Thus, you see, I am in clover,
And am still expecting lots of fun.

Three weeks of work, then away
For another glorious holiday,
Envious, you, I want not to make,
For you'll have four days, I'll have eight.

On Sunday I return with fear,
For I am not full of good _____?
This is getting rather low,
So, for once, I'll go slow.

 Please don't think of me next week – it may spoil your holiday to think of anybody working.
 Hoping the weather keeps fine for you, and that you all have a most enjoyable time (don't go in a speedboat),
    Yours very sincerely,
     Leonard.
Please remember me to rest of family.
  + cheer (Not Beer)

*

101/103 Burdett Road,
Bow,
London. E.3.
19-7-39

Dear Lily,
      Many thanks for your letter, which I received on Monday. I arrived home safe sound AND SOBER at 9.45 on Sunday, my total asset being the clothes I wore, a small suitcase half-full of rock, and 5 1/2d. (That's why I was sober). Work is (as usual), ~~lousy~~ lovely !!!*?
Please not newspaper cutting which is enclosed.
      As there is rather a lot of news, I have edited two special papers, which are enclosed, and I hope you will find them interesting.
      I hope that you enjoy the remainder of your holiday as much as I did, although, perhaps, in not the same way. I was very nearly broke,
                yours sincerely
                Leonard.

(Enclosed)

DOYLES NEWS FLASHES
<u>Editor:-</u> L. Doyle, esq.   <u>Reporter:-</u> L. Doyle, esq.
<u>Printer:-</u> L. Doyle, esq   <u>Publisher:-</u> L. Doyle, esq
      <u>Owner:-</u> L. Doyle, esq.

HECTIC SCENES AT GROUP-SHEET COUNTER.
Gory battle with tickets:- Francis. V Pearsone Richardson in 15 min. Fight.
      A dreadful scene was to be witnessed in the group-sheet counter on Saturday, 15 July, when Pearson (junior) attacked Richardson with the ticket box, the result being disasterous to the tickets and Richardsons head. At this point, common enemy of P and R (Francis) entered, P and R immediately united to ward off attack by F, but failed. F, in heat of battle reported aforesaid P and F to the miles bird, who

made them collect tickets from floor. P and F had busy weekend filing the tickets as homework. (They had to take tickets home, file them to vault by 8.35am., 10/7/39)

THE VAULT ART EXHIBITION.
There is a fine postcard exhibition in vault. Cards form various members of B.T.H. adorn all shelves. Cards are of both highbrow and vulgar type (mostly vulgar). One artiste, Miss L. Smith, is said to be commended for her fine views and scenes of Margate, but public (Mr. Colover) says it prefers lower type of card with comic (?) pictures and vulgar sayings. He wishes S. Smith would send some low cards, so that he may have vulgar laugh. One artiste in particular, Miss V. Charlton, should be commended on her low jokes.

UNWANTED VISITOR.
Mr. Richardson has acquired an unfortunate habit of entering vault during dinner-hour.

DREADFUL OPERATION ON MR. GLOVER
We regret to announce that Edwin Samuel Glover (Sammy, for short) had a painful dental operation on Tuesday, when one of his molars was removed, causing great physical pain to aforesaid victim. We are pleased to report, however, that he is making satisfactory progress.

No further bulletins will be issued.

AMAZING SCENE IN No1 BUILDING
There was an astounding scene, on Monday morning, in No1 Bldg., when a member of General Machines recommenced work after 1 week vacation. The heroeic member was affectionately greeted by his friends, who had fits when he started work at 8. o'clock sharp.

PRIVATE ANNOUNCEMENTS. (2d per word.)
Mr. E. S. Glover wishes it to be known to Miss L. Smith that he does not commence his holiday until 29 July,

and she will therefore have the pleasure – or otherwise – of seeing him for 5 days (except Friday) in the vault, before he leaves for his vacation.

WEATHER FORECAST FOR S.E. ENGLAND AND MARGATE.
For all this week:- Rain, hail, thunderstorms and gales.
Further <u>outlook:-</u> Rotten

THAT'S   ALL   FOR   NOW.

*

SEE IF YOU CAN OPEN THIS WITHOUT TEARING.

> 101/103 Burdett Road,
> Bow. E.3.
> 21-7-39

Dear Lily,
     I thought I had better write and let you know that I am still alive and kicking – but only just. After such a holiday as I had, WORK comes as a terrible, heart-rending shock to my fragile physique. I am now looking forward to August, when I hope to get in touch with a friend of mine who belongs to the Surrey and Sussex gliding club, and ask him if he can show me – and perhaps, a friend – over the club.

     I hope you enjoyed reading my news-sheets. I am very, very, sorry my weather forecast was so accurate, but I can't help being clever, can I? (Somebody who is reading this has just passed a rude remark re last line. Will you please excuse me for one moment? Thanks! *!?**stars.

     I have now bashed him up. Wheres that spinach? Ah! Now I feel better, To continue;-

     I am sorry to see that the weather has declined recently, and hope it improves before you return.

     I am looking forward to your instauration (wot a werd!), although I know that you are hating it. I can think of nothing more to say, so, wishing you a very pleasant journey home – and may the lemonade at 'halfway pull-up' be excellent –

> yours sincerely
> Leonard.

W.O.T. – Written on Thursday
P.O.F – Posted on Friday
W.R.Y.O.S. – Will reach you on Saturday.
G.P.O. – General Post Office.

(*Undated letter 9*)

Dear Lily,
        You might be interested to know that:-
On Saturday, July 29, the Granada, Willesden, is once again to be honoured by the patronage of Mr. B. L. Doyle, who, it is hoped, will be accompanied by Miss L. Smith.
        If Miss S. will be at the Granada not later than 1.15p.m and not earlier than 1.14p.m., Mr. D will meet her there and escort her to the auditorium
        Will Miss S. please let Mr. D know if this arrangement suits her, either (a) by a note, or, (b) to save time and trouble, by just writing the letters "O.K." on the top of the front page of a newspaper or periodical, and placing it in a prominent position in front of Mr. D.
        Yours sincerely,
        Leonard.

P.S. – Next time I will not be so circumlocutory, or use the art of circumlocution. I will just say, "Will you come to the flicks?"

*

>   B.L.Doyle
>   c/o Mrs.Masters,
>   20 Hayes Road,
>   Horns Cross,
>   Greenhithe,
>   Kent.
>   (wot an address)
>   10.0P.M.   7-8-39

Dear Lily,
    I intend to have a nice, quiet(?) easy (?) holiday here, and I know some excellent country around this place.

    After a gentle hint from me, my Aunty and Uncle wondered if you would like to be our guest on Sunday, 13 August. Now for my usual sermon:-

    I would, of course, very much like you to come, BUT, if you have other engagements, or do not wish to come (and I warn you, the journey here may not be a very pleasant one, and will take 70-100 mins., 'praps more), please do not be afraid to say so: I will in no way be offended. If you accept this invitation, and the weather is fine, I'll take you on a 2~~0~~0 mile ~~route march~~ walk. You will, of course, have dinner, tea – and if you arrive early enough – breakfast with us.

    If you have any films left in your camera, then I advise you to bring it, as there are opportunities for excellent snapshots here.

    Enclosed on a separate sheet are instructions on how to get to this 'ere place.
>   Yours very sincerely
>   Leo (the Lion).

P.S. – Please excuse pencil-work, as I am running out of ink. Once more, my address is:
   20 HAYES RD.,
      HORNS CROSS,
         GREENHITHE, KENT.

*

c/o Mrs. Masters
20 Hayes Road,
Horns Cross,
Greenhithe,
Kent,
9-8-39

Dear Lily,

Many thanks for the prompt reply which you gave to my letter, and I am pleased to say that, if you wish, a modification can be made to the arrangement for next Sunday, as follows:-

After another gentle hint from me, my aunty and uncle thought it would be a lot more enjoyable if you came down on Saturday and stayed the night with us. If you can do this – and I hope you can – it will be possible for us to visit Gravesend (attractions:- The Gasworks, Tilbury docks and river traffic), and Rochester (attractions:- Charles Dickens museum, Rochester Castle, the Cathedral, river Medway and, if in luck, some of the largest military and commercial flying-boats in England)

If you leave your home at 1.0p.m. you should arrive here between 2.30 and 3.0. Please note that you will have to obtain single tickets on the railway, as returns are available for day of issue only. Get a return on the coach, however; the return journey with these can be made at any time. Please note that the 'destination' board on the front of the coach will be GRAVESEND, and make sure you get on the right one, because there are about six other green-line coach routes that pass through the Elephant & Castle. (It is usually referred to just as 'the Elephant') also, don't forget to bring your sleeping-kit.

It rained yesterday evening, and I got a trifle wet, being, at the time, miles from anywhere: but whats the odds, so long as your 'appy?

The new ship, ~~Maure Mauretan~~ – I am afraid I can't spell the name, so I'll write it as it's pronounced – Mawretanya – will pass down the river near here on her way from King George V docks to the open sea on Friday ar'ernoon, an' I 'ope ter git some snaps of 'er.

There was a mimic air battle over here last night, and in theory we have all been blown to smithereens. Will you please let me have your reply, telling me what time you intend to leave your home on Saturday, as soon as possible, as, according to the news last night, letters and parcels may be delayed in the post, owing to the Black-Out.
      yours very sincerely
       Leonard
P.S. – I hope my plan of the Elephant is accurate, as it is drawn entirely from memory, and it is four years since I was last there.

1

SECTION A. ROUTE
1. By met. Train, from Neasden to Baker Street. (15-20 mins)
2. Thence, by Bakerloo line, direct to ELEPHANT & CASTLE (it's the same line we went to Waterloo on) (12-15 mins)
3. At Elephant & Castle, get GREEN LINE coach. (Route No A1 or A2. Ascot-London to Gravesend.) The coaches stop in St.GEORGES ROAD, and I believe the ''stop' board is just outside a dairy.(45-55 mins). See map below.

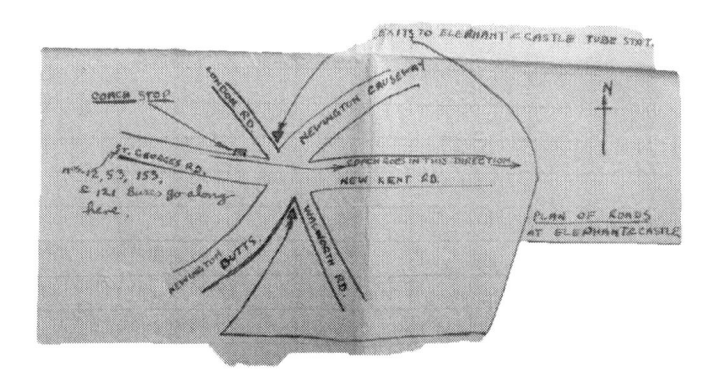

SECTION B. TICKETS
1. See if you can get a return right from Neasden to the Elephant & Castle. If this is not possible, take a return to Baker Street, and then a single to the Elephant.
2. When on the coach, as for a return to HORNS CROSS. If the conductor does not know where it is, tell him it's just before you get to Greeenhithe. The return fare will be about 2s/5d. Ask the conductor to let you know when you get to Horns Cross. Actually, It's about 2 miles past the town of Dartford. You will easily know when you get to Dartford by the 'AA' signs. Actually, you alight nearly opposite the 'Bull' (pub) at Horns Cross. THERE IS ALSO A 'BULL' (pub) stop at DARTFORD, so be careful not to make a mistake.

I will meet you where the coach stops, and thence escort you to my country seat. 'Hem. If, for any reason, I am not there, them below is thumbnail plan showing you how to get to Hayes Road.

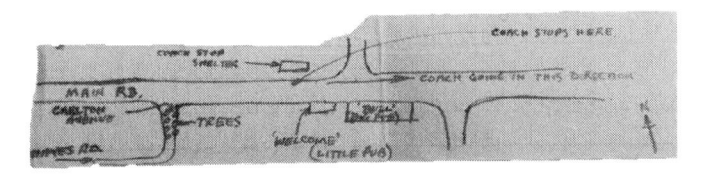

3
SECTION C   TIME.

It will be best to start as early as you possibly can – preferably not later than 8.15, and earlier if you can manage it.
The coaches run approx. every 30 mins., and I am afraid I can give you no time table.
So, you see, you may have to wait half an hour for a coach, if you are unlucky.
Will you please let me know what time you intend to leave your house, then I will know (approx) what time to be waiting for you?

We will leave here for the return journey at about 7.0pm., and I will see that you get home no later than 9.0p.m.

    sincerely hoping that you can come,
        your etc.
          Leonard.

*

                              c/o Mrs. Masters
                              20 Hayes Road,
                              Horns Cross,
                              Greenhithe,
                              Kent,
                              England,
                              The Earth,

                              10-8-39

Dear Lily,
          Well, that's nearly half a page filled up already. I thought I had better let you know that I received your letter at 8.30 this morning, opened it at 8.31 and read it at 8.32. After that I got up.
          When I finished putting on my boots (at 10.30) I wrote this, and I had better hurry because the post goes at 11.0.
          I will be waiting at the garden-gate-sorry, that's the old-fashioned version – I'll be waiting at the Green-Line coach stop between 2.25 and 3.45p.m. on Saturday, and, hoping you have a smooth journey (but you wait 'till you see some of the hills),
                    yours very sincerely,
                    Leonard.

                              *

(*Undated letter 10*)

Dear Lily,
        Have you any suggestions for Saturday or Sunday? If so, please let Mr. L. Doyle hear of them. For the best suggestion received by Friday, Sept.15, a prize of 6 fag cards, 4 marbles and a new farthing will be presented by the Rt. Hon. Lord Fitz-boozam on 30 Feb., 1978. There are no consolation prizes. Closing date for the competition is 1.22p.m, 15 Sept.
        The only thing L. Doyle can think of is to meet L. Smith at the Marble Arch, time 1.30, on Sept.17 (Sun), and then have a boat out on Serpentine, all journeys should be made by road, as rail services are curtailed; but L. Doyle would be pleased to hear of any other "outing" suggestions.
        Yours very sincerely,
      ~~Len~~ (still can't spell me name)

        Leonard

*

(Undated letter 11)

Dear Lily;-

<u>suggestions for Saturday.</u>
By Doyle.
<u>If weather be fine</u>:-
Regents Park, boat for two. You row.
<u>If weather be otherwise</u>:-
Some Sinema somewhere.
<u>Time</u>: - 1.15 p.m.
<u>Place</u>: - Bus stop, as per before.
above suggestions are subject to alteration by either party.
<u>Please note</u>:- air raids and war scares prohibited.

yours

very

sincerely

Leonard

(and that's filled the page up.)

*

*Len and Lily,
1939*

*Lily with Len's father,
Archibald, 1939*

*Len (playing the fool!) with his father,
Archibald, to his left, 1939*

The Terry's Chocolate Assortment box, where the letters were stored, with the note which was found at the bottom of the box.

Over 70 letters; many still in their envelopes, and postcards.

1940

(Undated letter 12)

Dear Lily,
      Owing to the international situation, it may be necessary to alter our plans for tomorrow.
      If the evacuation of London continues over tomorrow, transport may prove to be difficult: I thought it advisable therefore, to let you know that it might be best to visit some local cinema or place of entertainment, and to postpone the inspection of the zoo to a not-to-far-distant-date (assuming peace will prevail)
      Of course, if transport facilities on Saturday are normal, we will certainly visit the zoo. It is best, I think, to let you know of the above modifications beforehand, i.e. (that is,) now; it will not, I hope, "put you out" in any way.
      I will meet you, in any case, as per revious arrangement, at the bus stop at 1.15.
      If we do have to visit some local place, or, in other words, if transport is abnormal, I promised my parents I will leave for home almost immediately I leave the aforesaid local place.
      Hoping that Hitler will be haunted for the rest of his life by pink frogs with green legs and long tails with warts on,
                  Yours very sincerely
                    ~~Lenard~~ (I can't spell my
                              name right yet)

            Leonard

*

                              3rd Bench,
                              Embankment,
                              London W.C.I.
              Telephone: Disconnected (5 lines)
                              30.7.40

Dear Lily,
        As I am in a hurry, and can't fink of nuffink to say, will you please telephone me up at exactly 6.30 on Thursday?
                              Yours sincerely,
                              Len. (alias Lord Haw-
                                             Haw)

*

101, Burdett Road,
Bow. E.3.
28-8-40

Dear Lily,
    Owing to these night air-raid alarums (and it is alarum, not alarm), I, being on night shift, have recovered from my tiredfullness, and Eddie and myself are prepared to give you a lesson on riding the cycle next Sunday. We would like to go into the country around the north of London, chorley Wood and aylesbury way, etc., and we hope you know the way. Have you got, or could you borrow a cycle map of this district? If you will please phone me at 6.30pm on Friday, we will arrange the time of meeting, etc. If there is an air-raid alarum at that time, then phone me at 7.15pm on Saturday, and if you cannot get through then, try again at 8.0am on Sunday (our phone was blown to the floor when a bomb exploded near us last Saturday night).

    Eddie told me what a careless rider you are, knocking old men, woman and children down, turning right when you should turn left, and not giving any signals, etc. I'll learn you on Sunday.

    Poor old Eddie had a tooth out on Monday evening, then had to stay in the shelter for six hours Monday night.

    Hoping to see you on Sunday (in slacks),
Yours sincerely
Len.

P.S. I intend to sleep all day on Saturday, in case I have to get up Saturday night.

*

101 Burdett Road,
Bow. E.3.
5-9-40

Dear Lily,
    I intend, once again, with the help of Mr. Glover, to attempt an invasion of the country lanes north of London next Sunday, air raids, rest and sleep, etc. permitting.
    We will call on you (I hope) at about 9.45 (I hope), when (I hope), starting back for home at about 2.0pm (I hope). The transport will be two cycles and one old iron. (some hope). Assuming and hoping you will be able to come,

I remain,
yours hopefully,
B. Len. D

P.T.O

P.S – air Raid Warning at 9.20
9.27 – nine bombs dropped in quick succession, 650 yards away
9.30 – violent gunfire for 90 secs
10.20. several Nazis circling overhead intermittent gunfire
10.30 – Five heavy salvos of bombs about 800 yds away
11.0 – Nazis 'plane in trouble overhead: only one motor running
11.5 – About 10 bombs drop all around us. Plane is evidently jettisoning cargo.
12.30 – Nazi bomber and British fighter heard hunting each other.
1.0 – alls quiet
1.30 – more enemy aircraft heard.
1.30 – 2.0 about 10 bombs dropped, but probably about 1 to 2 miles away.
3.0 one heavy bomb dropped about 600yds away.
5.0 all clear, but searchlights still out.
5.3 Enemy 'plane overhead, everybody takes cover again
5.4 – Four bombs dropped, but about 3 miles away, Also gunfire.

5.8 Raid warning sounded again: several bangs in distance. Bombs or guns?
5.55 – all clear sounded.
9.0 –Air raid warning. 9.12- Enemy aircraft overhead. 9.14 – bombs dropped in distance. 9.15 – Extremely heavy gunfire.
9.15 – Bugger the raids, I'm posting this letter.
PLEASE NOTE: - If Saturday night is like this, I won't come on Sunday.

*

13 Gorings Mead
Horsham,
Sussex.
26-10-40

Dear Lily,
    I have safely arrived at my destination. I got an express train from Victoria, stopping at only three stations on the way here. I would have got here in 50mins, had not, by some unfortunate mischance an oil bomb dropped on the line during one of the morning alerts.
    We were held up for 1 hour.
    I went out, to a large natural park, this afternoon, accompanied by my sister. It poured with rain, and she was chased by a cow and I fell down a rabbit hole. Otherwise, we had a fine time. When I got back to Gorings Mead, I gave all the evacuated kids (four of them) a pick-a-back and box on their ears.
    The next item on the programme was to take my mother to a little teashop in the town, and we each had an afternoon tea.
    The waitress there was just like the tea, very nice, very tasty, very sweet. I do wish my mother had not been with me, 'cos tea for two is rather expensive when you pay for both, mother did.
    It would have been a lot cheaper if she had paid for me only, and stayed outside herself, especially as the tea was very nice, very tasty and <u>very</u> sweet.
    The countryside around here is delightful, and the houses in the town (there are five only in which I am interested – the Green Man, Oliver Cromwell, Red Cow, Black Hen and Wickam) are very comfortable. The lemonade is excellent.
    I wish I could squeeze you down here, I mean, squeeze you in down here, but I'll do my best to fix us up for one week end. I am sure you will like it here, and I know that I'll like you here, too.
    I must close now, good luck, and may you have a safe night.

yours very sincerely
Len.

P.S. My sister wishes to be remembered to you, so does Lil.

N.B.- I'm having a fine time here, but the medicine the doctor gave me is lousy, and mother makes me have it, I can't pour it down the drain.

*

13 Gorings Mead,
Brighton Rd,
Horsham,
Sussex.
28/10/40.

Dear Lily,

    A few lines to let you know how I am getting on down here. Yesterday (Sun) morning I walked to a neighbouring village with my mother, sister ('gor bless 'er) and Lil. I absolutely tired them out, lost them twice, made out I knew the way when I didn't, and mucked them about in general.

    The walk, which was supposed to be 4 miles, I managed to turn into 7 miles (and uphill most of the way). I thoroughly enjoyed myself, and I hope they did, too. After having refreshments (lemonade and water) we returned home to dinner. It was lovely and muddy out. After dinner I went up to St.Leonards forest with the evacuees, and we hunted for chestnuts. On the average, each of us fell off the tree into the mud twice. We returned home slightly dirty, and, of course, I got chewed up for the whole lot of us. I get blamed for everything. I wish you were down here to enjoy the fun and take half the blame.

    I am afraid I will not be able to take you out on Sat., as I have just realised that I will have to visit the doctors on Sat. afternoon, to get my signing off certificate.

    We will definitely go out the Sat. afterwards, though. (Heil Hitler, him permitting). I expect I will see you on Mon. evening.

    I have good reason to believe it will be possible for you and I to spend the week end here on 23 Nov.

    We will arrive down here at about 10.0am on Sat., and arrive home at about 12.0 midday on Mon. (I hope.) I am assuming you can get the required time off work. We will go to church on the Sunday. A terrific dogfight is going on overhead (time, 4.45p.m.). We saw 18 raiders pass over towards London at about 2.45p.m. We saw 16 returning, chased by 10 Spitfires at 2.52p.m. My neck aches through screwing my head upwards so much.

My mother and I were going to walk through the large natural park (Den Park) this afternoon, but when we got there, there was a cow the other side of the stile, and mother refused to go any further. So I got over the stile, to chase the cow away, only it was'nt a cow, but a bull, and he chased me.

Tomorrow we go to the cinema, where there are no bulls which look like cows 'till you get near them, only you did'nt get near 'em, I did. We went to a different teashop this time, where some old frump served us and I paid.

Horsham is now classed as a reception area except for those people who can find their own billets.

Mother is not going to have that cottage, as they have to walk 5 miles to any shop, but my sister and Lil may have it instead.

I sleep upstairs (in bed) with Dennis, and we have a pillow fight before we go to sleep, at 1a.m. and in the morning before we get up.

I may change my lodgings again, as Mrs.Swaly still wants to charge me 27/6 per week, although I am only there 5 days per week.

29/10/40

This moring (Tue), a barrage balloon (loose) drifted over the town from the direction of London. An aeroplane is circling above it, waiting before it drifts clear of the town before shooting it down.

As there is no more news, I must close now,
    Moja Kochana, velly much
        yours very sincerely,
            Len.
POSTED TUE. MORN.

*

>13 Gorings Mead
>(or Hitlers alleyway),
>Brighton Rd,
>Horsham
>Sussex
>30/10/40

Dear Lily,

    Received your letter today, and was very sorry to hear that Francis had been bombed out, and of Ada's loss. Will you please convey my sincere sympathy to Francis?

    We are not entirely without excitement down here, because at about 4.0pm. yesterday (tue), a messerschmitt 109 (single seater) had a machine-gun dual with a Spitfire at about 400ft above our heads. The Spitfire won, the messerschmitt crashing in a field about 3 miles away. We saw it come down. The pilot was pulled out with all his trousers alight, and had to have both his legs amputated. He died in hospital late on tue. night.

    We have a cannon shell from the ME109 which fell in the street. It was announced on the radio, and published in the paper that:- "a single-seater enemy fighter was shot down in flames near Horsham, Sussex, after machine gunning workers in the fields."

    I am looking forward to seeing you again, but am most certainly NOT looking forward to returning to London, after having been in such delightful surroundings as are here. Once more, I intend to change my lodgings (or have I told you before?)

    I went to the flicks this afternoon ((with my mother:I am behaving myself this time, and havn't taken any strange girls out, and don' intend too. (collapse of reader))

    Please remember me to Eddie and give my kind regards to Elsie, Sylvy (is that spelt right?) and you mother and father.

    The prospect of you and I spending a weekend down here (23 Nov) are improving, as Lil is returning to London with me on Saturday. If, however, she returns here on or before 23 Nov, then the prospects diminish.

    I got mother in a fix yesterday when we went out for a walk.

I coaxed her through one field of cows, into an empty field, then she got scared, because the field ahead also had cows in; if she reversed she had to go through cows, and if she went forward she had to go through cows. I coaxed her forward, but the field after THAT had bulls in it. Then the siren went, and about 20 Nazis passed over, and mother nearly passed out ('cos a bull looked at her). Everything came alright in the end, however, but the story is too long to tell here, owing to the paper shortage.
There is no more news I can think of,
yours with a _____, (word of 4 letters)
very sincerely,
Len.
POSTED ON THUR, AFTERNOON, 31/10/40
all clear went at 10.30pm. last night, it's pouring with rain this morn.

*

1941

101 Burdett Rd,
Bow. E.3.
21/1/41

Dear Lil,
    Just a few words (167 to be precise) to inform you that I arrived home safely at 4.40pm. on Sunday. (The picks don't open 'till 7.0pm)
    I started work on a new bunk for father on Sunday night, but did not get far as I had no suitable timber. My dear Pater is going to buy some wood on Thursday, and I will therefore be extremely busy with hammer, screwdriver, saw, etc., on Thursday night and several nights thereafter.
    It is very thirsty work. (nuff said!)
    Father has a cold, and retired early to bed last night (Monday).
    I dosed him with hot milk, ETC, and aspras.
    I am going to repeat the cure again tonight. My work is proceeding SmOoThLy.
There is no more news I can think of at present.
Hoping your feet are warmer than they were at 11.30a.m. last Sunday (you had better wear two pairs of ankle socks next time),
                      Yours always,
                          Len.

*

101 Burdett Rd,
Bow. E.3.
Mon. 27-1-41

Dear Lily,
   Just a few (?) lines to let you know how I am getting on.
   I arrived home, safe, sound and sober (in future letters I'll just put S.S.S to save paper, and ink) at 7.50 on Saturday evening.
   And here is the rest of the news, gathered and written by Leonard B. Doyle (copywrite reserved, except the rhymes, which may be reproduced on any country on this Earth-or off it – at a small fee. Apply to Len. B. Doyle, Burdett Rd. Business:- at all times when public houses and other places of liquid refreshment are CLOSED.) News is read by Lilian Rose Smith.

Some Literature.
   There was a young lady called Lily,
   Who once climbed a tree and got dizzy,
   She wanted to cough, and nearly fell off,
   Into the arms of some silly old billy.

BOY MEETS INCAPACITATED CHARGE-HAND.
   An interesting scene was to be witnessed at Baker Street tube station at 7.45a.m. on Sunday, 26 Jan., '40, when a young gentleman going to work – to be presise, Mr. B. L. Doyle, the famouse engineer and writer – happened to see his charge-hand, Mr. William Riley in a semi-intoxicated condition.
   It appears that Mr. Riley (whose home is in Neasden), had been out on the tiles all night, retiring underground at 2a.m. He was accompanied by another gentleman (also squiffy), and an employee of the B.T.H.
   Mr. Riley, who was due to work that morning, warmly welcomed the great engineer, and the three of them proceeded on their journey in a northbound met. train to the tune of "I won't get home to the morning". On arriving at the

B.H.T. Mr. Riley came in for five minutes, requested Mr. Doyle to work until 12.30a.m., and then go home.
 Mr. Riley them retired to bed, and was not seen until Mon. morn. when he came in perfectly sober and with a large bump on his forehead, which he received from his wife as thanks for staying out all night.

SECT.9 INSPECTED BY INSPECTORS
 Section 9 was, on Monday last, honoured by a visit from those two illustrious personalities, Messrs. Glover and Lasham. After wasting 1 hour of the sections time, i.e. after speaking to Mr. Doyle for 1 hour, they informed him of a lunch for the apprentice ass. which was to be held at the Norfolk Hotel in 15/2/41 (tickets, 3?- and all jokes to be kept clean until the B.T.H. manager, Mr. T. Hands has departed), and requseted Mr. Doyle's presence. The invitation was gratefully received by the aforesaid Mr. Doyle.

PUZZLE
 Fill in the missing letters. Solution on page 29, column 3.

There was a ___ ___ called ___
Who was really a nice bit of frilly,
But whenever we met,
She will get c___d f___t,
Which made poor Lily get quite chilly.

IMPORTANT
 Mr. B. L. Doyle will call on Miss L. Smith on Friday, to receive a gold medal for poets. In the meantime, he is taking a course of "How to defend oneself against ferocious females".

MORE LITERATURE
A certain girl I cuddled
Went walking through some puddles.
She got very wet (nearly up to her neck)
And is still rather fizzled and fuzzled.

And that is the end of the News Bulletin. Another will appear on Feb.29, 1941. Goodnight, dear reader, goodnight.

>   yours always,
>   Len.

P.S. (perfectly sober)

PLEASE DON'T BE TOO HARD ON ME ABOUT THE POEMS.

*

101 Burdett Rd
Bow. E.3.
Sat, 8/2/41
3.0pm

Dear Lily,
    Just a line to let you know I could not come round on Friday or Saturday, as I had a touch of the flue, and did not go to work on Thur, Fri or Sat.
    I am all right now, however (I only had a touch of the flue – Not COLD FEET-), and will turn up at work on Monday, although I may not come round to see you 'till Friday. Alls well. Nothing else to report.
    Yours sincerely, Len

*

101 Burdett Rd,
Bow. E.3

18/2/41

My Dear Lily,
    Just a line to let you know I will not be up to see you on Friday, as I will want to spend all Friday evening preparing for Saturday. I will, however, come to see you on Friday, 28/2/41.
    When I register, it will be as a flight mechanic (if they accept them with specs.). If they don't
"   "   "   ", then as a Radio operator. I shall probably be slung into the army anyway.
    Have you noticed in radio jokes, etc., how the R.A.F, is always praised, the army treated like a lot of nitwits, and the navy completely ignored?
    I will probably be going out with Eddie and Bartlett on Sun, 2/3/41, but I may be able to squeeze you on – I mean squeeze you IN – on Sat. 1/3/41.
    The gentlemen upstairs dropped one or two big ones around here last night, and got a delightful little fire going near the back Gasworks. I hear you had a bomb at the back of you, too.
    Nothing else to report,
        Yours always,
            Len.
P.S. I am leaving this letter in an addressed envelope (unstamped) for dad to post. I hope it gets to you stamped.

*

101 Burdett Rd,
Bow. E.3
Sun. 9/3/41

My dear Lily,
    I received a letter from my mother Saturday night, stating that:-
    "I expect it will be all right for you to bring Lily, but we are waiting for a camp bed to be put in, and some more blankets from the billeting officer."
    In other words, they will be very pleased to see you if you don't mind sleeping on the floor with an old coat over your anatomy.
    I am endeavouring to send the sheets, pillows etc. by train to Slinfold Post Office, to be collected there.
    The address of this bungalow is:-
Lydwick Lodge,
Hayes Lane,
Slinfold (nr.Horsham)
Sussex.
    If we get on a Petworth bus at the Carfax, Horsham, Lydwick Lodge is only a minutes walk after alighting. These buses only run at 9.10am, 11.0am, 1.10pm, 3.10pm, 5.10pm and 7.10pm, however.
    There is another bus service, considerably more frequent, to Slinfold village, when we will have 1½ miles to walk after alighting.
    This should take us no longer that 20 mins. (Our average walking pace is about 6m.p.h – and I'm not kidding).
    Lydwick Lodge is 5 mins. walk from Slinfold Halt, and I am about to institute enquiries designed to find out the train service to this Halt. I will also see if I can get Dennis to meet us at Horsham station.
    There is, of course, one more method of reaching our destination – by Shanks Pony, from Horsham.
    The distance to Slinfold is about 6 miles, and I believe I know the way (here the reader laughs sarcastically).
    I would like to meet you at Neasden Station on Saturday at 12.50 precisely (and please don't be late).
    We may be able to get a train from Victoria at 1.30p.m. to arrive at Horsham by 3.0p.m., in which case we

will be able to catch the 3.10p.m. Petworth bus. We will return home Monday morning.

    So much for Horsham.

    I sincerely hope you got home safely on Saturday night.

    We had a hell of a night. The City, Aldgate, East Ham and this district copped it good and proper. About 200 incendiaries were dropped in Burdett Road. All were of the explosive type. No major fire developed, and the only casualty was a man who was knocked down and seriously hurt by a fire pump.

    I cycled to East Ham this morning, and called on Mrs. L. Martin.

    She will be seeing Vera Lynn in about a fortnight, and will try to get me two tickets for the Palladium. Leslie (in the navy) has, up to January, visited Nova Scotia (Canada), Bermuda (W.Indies) and Capetown (S.Africa). He seems to be getting around a bit.

    He called on an uncle of his at Capetown. Talk about come in and see me sometime!

    I may call and see you on Friday. If I don't call, I will let you have a postcard telling you everything is O.K.

    If you don't receive a postcard by Friday, 'phone me on Frid. night at exactly 7.10p.m. (ADV.3756).

    Jusqu'a samedi, adieu, mon amoreux,
                            Len.

PS. Harry passed A1, and will probably be an R.A.F. policeman.

*

101 Burdett Rd,
Bow. E.3

Don't know the date,
but it Wednesday.

Dear Lily,
  Just a line to let you know I have, what I am afraid is a great disappointment for you. It is not possible for us to go to Horsham this week – end, as my mother has decided that the bungalow is not suitable after all. It is rather damp and too lonely. My respected father is therefore, going to Horsham this week end instead of us, and I will stay at home to do the washing. I expect we can go out on Sat., though.
  I am very sorry to let you down like this, and will try not to let it occur again.
  I expect we can go to Horsham in about 3 weeks time.
<u>Will see you on Friday.</u>
  P.I.A.R   Yours sincerely
(posted in air raid)   Len

*

101 Burdett Rd.,
Bow.E.3.

Frid. morn.

My dear Lily,
    I am sorry I could not come along on Friday evening, as I had an accident at work on Thursday a heavy casting falling on my foot.
    The ambulance people bungled the job completely. The accident happened at 11a.m., the worst injury being to the big toe. Yet they only put a little oil on it, and told me to carry on as usual.
    All was o.k 'till after grub, when my toe swelled to twice its normal size and was extremely painful. Of course, I had my boot off.
    Bill called the ambulance man, yet it was not until 4.0pm that I was shifted, by motor trolley, to the ambulance room.
    Then someone woke up to the fact that matters were getting bad, and hot bandages etc, were applied. Then (what I consider their greatest blunder), they gave me a pass-out at 5.0pm., and told me to get home as quickly as possible. I asked for crutches without result, but managed to obtain in the end, a shoe several sizes too large.
    The journey home was torment, and made my foot a lot worse. Things are improving slightly now, though. <u>I shall expect you here on Sunday at 2.0p.m. sharp</u>

Love,

    Len

*

101 Burdett Rd.,
Bow. E3.

3/6/41.   9.30p.m.

Dearest Lily,
             Please excuse this writing as I have got hold of a lousy pen and the cats been drinking the ink. I am looking forward to crawling into my bunk in 30 mins. time, and reading a bloodthirsty story before going to sleep. I feel browned off, chewed up, kicked about and sat upon (as you like listening to moans, I'm giving you some)
             Fish, groceries, vegitables clothing and boots have gone up so considerably that I cannot afford them.
             This thought so upset me that I went to the doctor. His fees had gone up 20 per cent., and medical supplies which he recommended were all up.
             I decided it would be better to pass out, but funeral costs, I found, were more than ever. (Evening news 3/6/41)
             Anyhow, to come down to brass tacks (although you can't even get them nowadays):-
             I will call for you at 1.0-1.15p.m. on Sat.
             I will want you to have the case ready as Dad will have to take it down to Horsham with him.
             You will come home with me on Sat. We may go to the pictures Sat. evening.
             On Sun I expect to have that debate (?) with the vicar of St. Marys, and so I will make Sunday arrangements with you on Sat. (You'll probably meet me at West End on Sun., and we'll have a look round there).
             That's all for now, except that the weathers rotten, and we might get an air raid shortly, 'cos the R.A.F. has bombed Berlin.
             So everythings lousy. Hoping this good man has cheered you up, and that this finds you as it leaves me,

yours with a crick on the neck and an ache
            all over,

Love,
                        Len.

P.S. – work went awful.
I can't find the bloodthirsty story.

                        *

101 Burdett Rd.,
Bow. E3.

16/6/41. (Mon).

My Dear Lily,
    A few lines to let you know that I will be having A.R.P practise on Friday evening, and will not, therefore, be home to your house until about 7.0-7.30 p.m.
    Hoping you don't ache too much and that your oojamaflip isn't too sore,
        Love,
        Len.

P.S. – I have bought my birthday book. That's 7s/6d, please. Tomorrow (is it one m or two? Toommorrow, twomorrow, or tomorrow?), anyhow, the day after today (or when today is yesterday), I am getting a 1s/6d book on dancing.

        *

101 Burdett Rd.,
Bow E.3.
Monday, 14/7/41.

My dear bit of fluff,
    Will you please be prepared to start from your house, for Horsham, at 7.30a.m (in the morn.) on Sat?
    I will meet you at the information office, Victoria station, at 8.20a.m. sharp.
    I am trying to get Sat. morning off. If there is any change to the above programme, I will call and see you Friday evening.

Please make a not to bring the following:-
1. Any bacon, butter, sugar + cheese ration you have
2. Your RATION BOOK
3. Your bathing costume.
4. All chocolate, grub + FAGS (I cant spell cigaretts) you can lay hands on.

    Cheerio, + lots of love,
    Len   x

P.E.P
    (Please excuse pencil)
P.S.R
    (Please send reply, so I am sure you have received this)

*

1942

                              101 Burdett Road.,
                                       Bow E.3.

                    Wednesday, 8th July 1942.

To my dearest Lily,
          Just a few short lines, my dear, in lieu of a
birthday card, to wish my darling many, many happy
returns for her twenty second birthday; and may the
years ahead bring her all the happiness and joy she
desires.
                    From Len,
her sweetheart, with all his love.

                              *

101 Burdett Road.,
Bow. E.3.

13/10/42

My Dearest Lily,
    I am afraid I will not be into work for a few days. I went to the doctors yesterday (Monday), and he told me my temperature was up considerably, and I had a 'flue' chill.
I feel a lot better today, however, and I hope to get up again on Thursday.
Harry went into hospital on Monday.
Please excuse my handwriting and the shortness of this letter, as I am sitting up in bed writing with a fountain pen, and the ink will insist upon flowing backwards, into the pen, instead forwards, out of it (as per sketch).

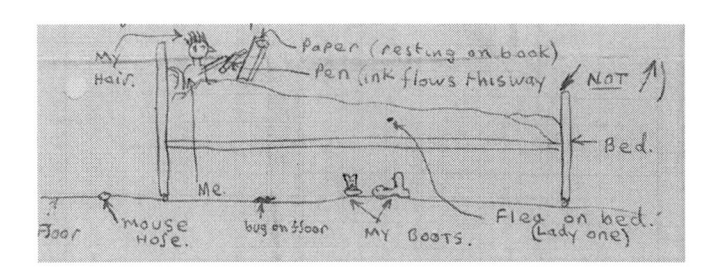

Cheerio, darling,
                         Len
P.S. – expecting you on Saturday.

*

                                            101 Burdett Road
                                            Bow. E.3

                                            14.10.42.

My dear sweetheart,
     Just a few lines to let you know how I am getting along dear. I have been feeling rather miserable since yesterday. It was not until I had posted your letter that I realised you had your half-day today, and had an opportunity of visiting me this evening (if your mother was well). Consequently, I have been very much looking forward all day to seeing you this evening, even though I know it is unlikely that you will come along, as I put "Saturday" on my last letter. It is now six o'clock, and you haven't turned up yet, I almost feel as if I could cry, I yearn to see you so much, having been on my own nearly all day.
     As you can see from the above, I feel pretty well down in the dumps (which is unusual for me), but expect I will get over it.
     I stayed in bed all day yesterday, and did not get up until 5 p.m. today, to have a wash. I feel rather weak, and am retiring again at about 7.30 p.m. My "flu" is a lot better. I cannot write much more at present; please excuse me for the hopeless mess I have made of this letter, as I feel slightly dazed (due to weakness, I suppose), and the pen will insist upon making little squiggles and wiggles which neither my hand nor mind can control.
     The worst is now over, and I expect I will feel immensely better + stronger tomorrow.
     I hope your mother is now O.K.
               Cheerio, darling,
                                                    Len
P.S. - on re-reading this letter, I see it rings a rather despondent note, but please dont get downhearted – I will be as good as new by Friday.

*

*Wedding Day,
10th Sept, 1944*

1947

1947

1948

75

Len, Lily and one year old Michael, 1950

1984

Len with great-grandson, 2003

1943

(On paper folded over to make a card)

         101 Burdett Road,
           Bow, E.3.

       For Friday, 9th July 1943.

To wish my darling
"Many Happy Returns"
with all of my love, and fondest wishes.

"Since you have your own dear place
Down in my heart each day,
You well deserve the love that comes
With this to you on your birthday."

      Len.

        *

101 Burdett Rd.,
Bow E.3.

Wed. 24/11/43.

My darling Lily,
To begin with, I wish you would tie a sensible !!@*-! Bow in my boots, so that I can undo the -----!! boots in fifteen minutes instead of thirty mins. I nearly went to bed with my boots on, on Sunday night. Mother stopped me just in time, and took my boots off for me. She undid the bows in about half a second. I suppose my useless efforts must have loosened them first.

I presume that our mutual friend, Mr. E. S. Glover has already informed you of our shopping expedition.

The stores seemed to have nothing in them except "Ladies underwear" departments. Anyhow, that's where we kept landing up. It must be some sort of instinct, I suppose.

Well, sweetheart, I have no idea whatsoever how I did in the I.E.E. English exam. It was a stinker.

I went to Stratford with my mum on Tuesday afternoon, to buy a raincoat, and I bought an overcoat. I now owe my mum £7-10s, and my mum owes my dad some too, but I don't think he'll get it.

I have now covered ground up to Wednesday.

I duly arrived at Ilford this morning, where the mayor of Ilford and the town band welcomed me. Having been conducted at Plessey's (1 1/2d bus fare), I reported at their employment office. The first thing they do is to note your height, colour of hair and eyes. They then take your photograph. I was patiently awaiting the issue of a coupon-free suit (with broad arrows), when they informed me the next item of the agenda was a medical exam.

The doctor sounds your chest, feels your body to see if your still warm, and if you can stand up – your IN!!

You can tell Eddie the first job they gave me (which will keep me busy for about 10 days) was a radio transmitting set as used in aircraft assembled with its component parts, etc, but not wired. I have to draw the wiring ASSEMBLY (for the fitter) and the DIAGRAM (for the electrician).

The office consists of three youths (17-21 yrs) who seem O.K. as draughtsmen, but know nothing whatsoever about the technical side, 1 boy (15 yrs) to run errands and make the tea. 1 junior draughtsman (22) with ord.nat.cert, 1 technician (30 yrs) who does'nt seem to know much, two girl tracers (very nice, but both married), a randy typist, and the BOSS. Then, of course, there's me.

No one seems to work very hard or care much whether they do the job right or wrong. When I get used to the job, I should be right on top.

Well, darling, I must close now.

All my love,

Len.

P.S. – Remember me to Beauchamp and tell him I'll hold a job open for him when I'm manager.

I could not find Snow, but expect I'll come across him before the weeks out.

Working hours are 8.30a.m to 5.30p.m. and I'm indoors by 6.10p.m.

*

101 Burdett Road,
Bow, E.3.

Tuesday, 7 Dec. 1943.

My dear sweetheart,
            Well, its Tuesday and I don't know what to write about. There have been no marriages, births or deaths to report since Monday. The price of beer has neither risen nor fallen, and the income tax is still high.
            Mother arrived home on Monday, as per expected, and gave the latest news of the BIG BOMBS that have been deposited at Horsham ---------- etc., etc.
            Well, darling, there is not much more to say, except that mother and father (Gawd bless 'im) send you their love.
            Cheerio, and all my love,
            Len
Xxxxxxxxxxxxxxxxxxxxxxxxxxxxxxxxxxxxxxxxxxxxxxxxx
xxxxx!!@*?!xxxxxxxxxxxxxxxx (Don't tickle
!!@*?!)xxxxxxxx
xxxxxxxxxxxxxxxxxxxxxx.

*

101 Burdett Road,
Bow. E.3.

Tuesday, 14 Dec 1943.

My darling Lily,
    Well its Tuesday again and there still aint nothing to write. I did two hours overtime tonight and did not arrive home until 8.15p.m., in time to hear the brains trust.

I had sum soop and bred and cheeze four me supper, wich was very injoyable becas I was very hungry. Yew sea, yoo are knot the ownly wen hoo spells diferetit, I kan doo it two.

Well sweetheart, I trust you will not take the above paragraph too much to heart. After all, I've got to fill this page up somehow.

I have now worked out my share of the beer at work. We have fifteen quarts of brown ail (I mean ale) and 1 bottle of whisky + 1 bottle of gin with no it.

I will be at Wembly Park station on Friday 17 Dec. 1943 at 7.20 – 7.30p.m.

Hoping you are in the best of health while I am in the best of spirits,

Cheerio darling,
Len.

P.S. – Ma and Pa send their love.

*

101 Burdett Road,
Bow E.3.

Tues. 22 Dec. 1943.

My darling sweetheart,
      Well its Tuesday again, and time for your weekly (or weakly?) news letter. Im thinking hard, dear, but there still is'nt much news, so I'll have to fill in the blank spaces by saying "I love you".
      Two of the bombs dropped on Monday fell on the railway shunting yards near Colborn Road Station (the arch you pass on the way to Victoria Park)
      I love you darling.
      I seem to be having all the luck lately, my fire-guard(guard/) (garud) (or gord) place at Plesses is in one of the cottages they own in Vicarage lane. There are proper beds, etc., in the bedrooms and downstairs is the cashier's office. I suppose they chose me because I am tall, dark honest-looking, trustworthy, conscientious and handsome. Or it may have been that I look such a brainless idiot that they thought "he can't do any harm, anyhow."
      Well, darling, I am looking forward to you seeing me on Sunday (I will be too drunk to see you), and I hope things are not too bad at home.
      I think your sweet, darling.
      Dennis is here and will probably stay until Christmas (being a communist, I would prefer to say 25 December 1943)
      Mother swore about the fish again yesterday.
      Will you please take note of the results of the Decem 25 draw.
      Well, sweetheart, cheerio for now,
            All my love,
            Len
      Raised to the power infinity.
Xxxxxxxxxxxxxxxxxxxxxxxxxxxxxx (Love)

*

101 Burdett Road,
Bow E.3.
Thur. 23 Dec. 1943.

Darling Lily,
        I expect you will be rather surprised at receiving this, but it is in lieu of a Christmas Card. Mother tried to get some cards, but could not do so.

        Here's to wishing my darling, from the bottom of my heart, a very happy Xmas and a peaceful new year that will bring fourth all her hopes and desires. Xxxxxxx

        Well, we have received your calendar, and mum and dad are very pleased with it. They have ask me to wish you, on their behalf, a happy Xmas and peaceful New Year.

        I am taking that big enamel mug mother had at Southwater, to work with me on Friday. Its to put my beer in.
        Cheerio for now sweetheart,
        Len.
Xxxxxxxxxxxxxxxxxxxxxxxxxxxxxxxxxxxxxxxxxxxxxxxxx
xx

*

1944

101 Burdett Road,
Bow. E.3.
Tue. 4 Jan. 1944.

~~Dear Madam~~
My darling Lily,
    I arrived home safely on Sunday, and after having supper, went to bed. Mother (Mrs. Doyle) is improving, and now gets up a few hours a day. I thought of you, darling, when the alert went on Sunday night. We all stayed in bed – Mother because she coud'nt stand up if she wanted to, me because it was lovely and warm and cosy, and dad because he was – what's that, mum? I must'nt write things like that about dad? All right, dad stayed in bed because he was sleepy.
    Well, dearest, I have piles of notes & homework to do, so I must close now.
Cheerio, sweetheart,
Len. Xxxxxx

*

101 Burdett Road,
Bow. E.3.
Tues. 11-1-44

My dearest,
      Well, its Tuesday again and time for my weekly news letter.
      I have been working very hard lately; up to 8.30p.m on Monday and 7.30p.m. tonight. Tomorrow I am booking tickets for Lyle, and I am looking forward to the dance on next – this – that? – Tuesday.
      I am afraid I cannot make news when there isn't any (I love you, sweetheart), so I will have to close soon. Please remember me to Tony Little and "the boys". Also the girls, but only the nice ones.
              Cheerio, darling,
                  Len.
              Xxxxxxxxxx

*

101, Burdett Rd.,
Bow. E.3.
Tues. 25 Jan. '44.

My Darling,
 Just a few lines to let you know we are all O.K. I went to the doctors last night, like a good boy, and received 1 bottle of medicine I had before.

 Well, I've been doing some problems tonight, darling, but have not got very far, and it has put me into a bad temper, because I don't like anything to beat me. Mother is just raving at me to have my chest rubbed; so I will soon have to close down.

 Stan (i.e. Mr. Snow) was presented with a son at 10.30a.m. on Sunday last. He said it looks like a little old man.

 Well, sweetheart, mother is still on at me (about clearing the table now), so I will really have to sign off.
 cheerio until Saturday, darling,
 All my love,
 Len
xxxxxxxxxxxxxxxxxxxxxxxxxxxxxxxxxxxxxxxxxxxxxxxxxxx
x

*

101 Burdett Road,
Bow. E.3.
Tues, 1 Feb. 1944.

My Darling Sweetheart,
    Well, here I am again, and feeling quite bright and perky. I was on fireguard today, rose at 6.0a.m. and arrived home 90 mins. ago (at (8.20, that is).
    Mother has had a letter from Horsham, asking her to go there when she can, and also saying that Aunty Ada would be pleased to see you and myself at any time we care to go there. (What a pity we can't go!)
    I am now getting quite used to sleeping in ladies underware, and certainly do sleep well when wearing the vest.
    Coming home on the trolleybus tonight, I passed two fires – one between Ilford and Stratford & t'other 'tween Stratford & Bow.
    I am afraid, darling, that I am now running out of thoughts – except, of course, to say "I love you, darling" – and so I will now have to close, my sweetheart,

Cheerio until Saturday,
All my love,
Len
Xxxxxxxxxxxxxxxxxxxxxxxxxxxxxxxxxxxxxxxxxxxxxxx
xx

*

101 Burdett Road,
Bow. E.3.
Wed. 2. Feb. 1944.

My Dearest,
    I received your letter this evening, and (needless to say) I am very, very sorry to see you so down in the dumps, my darling.
    If you wish, you may come over here on Thursday or Friday evening – you are always welcome, sweetheart – but I understand if you would rather stay at home with your mother.
    I will be doing overtime on Thursday, but, if you can come, please don't let me being on overtime stop you. Bang on the shutters if mother does'nt hear you at the door.
    We have two cushion covers (gold) only left, but dad is trying to get some more from the warehouse tomorrow – i.e. thursday.
    Well, my darling, there is not much more I can say – except, of course, "I love you, darling" – and so will soon have to close dearest.
    My first translation of your French was that "I aimed Beauchamp over France", but have now translated to read "I love you very much" – i.e. "Lily loves Len very much". Gee whiz!
    I love you, darling,

                Cherrio, all my love,
                        Len.
xxxxxxxxxxxxxxxxxxxxxxxxxxxxxxxxxxxxxxxxxxxxxxxxxx

P.S. – I feel almost normal now, and my cough is a lot better.

*

                                            101 Burdett Road,
                                                Bow. E.3.
                                            Tues. 8 Feb. 1944.

My Darling Lily,
                I have just returned from my I.E.E. meeting and had supper (stew & toast) after listening for two hours to Colonel Sir A. Stanley Anguin, D.S.O. M.C. (Military Cross or Master of ceremonies?). T.D. BSc ………. Etc talking about Progress in Telecommunications (long word that, - Telecommunications – if I can use it often enough in this letter, then I'll soon fill the space up, and at the same time give you a nice long letter to read. Telecommunications – I'll have to remember that word).
        Well, darling, mother bought my chocolate rations yesterday – 4 bars Frys chocolate cream & 4oz slab of plain. Owing to the lecture in Telecommunications, which made me hungry, there are now 2 bars of Frys chocolate cream & 1 – 4oz slab of plain.
        Old mother Riley is coming to the Plessey Co. in the lunch-time on, (I think) Feb.11, Friday, and it will be broadcast (not Telecommunicated) in "Workers Playtime"
        Well, dearest, I will now turn over as "Telecommunications" seems to have carried me through the previous page.
        I love you, darling.
        Mother sends her love.
        There appears to be no more intelligent news to communicate (NOTE:- If "Tele" is put in front of "communicate" it becomes "Telecommunicate")
        I really will have to close now, sweetheart, as it is time for my bed and mummy is calling me and daddy has just come in.
                        Ta – Ta for now, darling,
                            All my love,
                                            Len.
xxxxxxxxxxxxxxxxxxxxxxxxxxxxxxxxxxxxxxxxxxxxxxxxxxxxx
x

P.S. – The 2 bars of chocolate cream left, I'm trying very hard to save for you. TRYING….. TRYING……TRYING…… TRYING…….. TRYING……..TRYING…….. Tried.

*

101 Burdett Road,
Bow. E.3.
Tues. 15/2/44

My Darling,
Here is this weeks news letter, and this is B. L. Doyle writing it.

Flash1 – On Monday night, 14 Feb, thieves broke into Fishes shop at Peckham Park Road and, in spite of the fact that people were sleeping over the shop, cracked the safe and got away with £3000 in jewels and cash.

Well, dearest, I thought about you when the alert went on Sunday evening. We had a rather rough time, and a fair – size fire was started in the councils horse stables, just behind the Peoples Palace. Even dad stayed in the shelter for 10 whole minutes without going outside. We had "Lil & Alf" (sounds like two characters form Comic Cuts) with us.

I received a Valentine on the 14th, my sweetheart, but I cannot imagine who sent it. It has "Bow" postmark on the envelope, so I suppose it must be from one of my local female admirers.

It has lovely words, and I'm sure the person who sent it must be a real darling. It would make you quite jealous if you could see it, dear.

Well, darling, thats the lot for now, except to say that I'm working until 7.30p.m. every night this week except Thursday.

I love you, darling,
Cheerio!
Len

xxxxxxxxxxxxxxxxxxxxxxxxxxxxxxxxxxxxxxxxxxxxxxxxxxx

P.S. – am looking forward to seeing you on Sunday.

*

                                              101 Burdett Road,
                                              Bow. E.3.
                                              Tues. 22 – 2- 44

My Darling,
             Well, I'm still alive and kicking even though Sunday night was rather hectic.

Mother told me all about your adventures on Sunday while waiting for Wailing Winnie to whiz, and about dad banging on the door. She said you seemed to be rather pensive, so cheer up darling, we'll be together all next week end.

I thought P-'s was going up in flames at one time in the first raid when the gentlemen upstairs released a load of phosphorous bombs immediately overhead. Luckily there was a breeze up, and it blew the bombs (they fall rather slowly, and are alight coming down) just outside the factory area. There are four other chaps with me on fire guard. Someone suggested it would be a good idea if we put some of these bombs out (they were just outside our area), and we all agreed it was a jolly good idea, but no one seemed to say "I'll go". So for about fifteen minutes we all agreed it WAS a good idea, and by the end of that time the things had burnt themselves out, so we did'nt have to trouble after all.

Well, dearest, I would have liked you to have seen us when the alert went at 3.30a.m on Monday morning. The warning bells went in our shelter (there were 40-50 fireguards sleeping there), and after about two minutes, everyone was sitting up in bed swearing, cursing and blasting really good. It was a treat to hear it, as, in spite of the cold air, it seemed to warm the shelter up.

I expect you are tired of hearing about air raids now, my sweetheart, so I will change the subject.

Aunty Ada, Aunty Mabel and Lulu are coming up for the day on Wednesday.

I am looking forward to seeing you on Saturday, my darling, as I had you for such a short time on Sunday.

There is no more news at present, I'm afraid, except to say "I love you, darling", so cheerio & all my love,
                                              Len.

P.S. – For Pete's sake, hurry up and take your chocolate from the sideboard. The mental anguish I go through exercising my willpower is terrible.

     I want it so much that I think, if I only relaxed, that the chocolate would walk out of the sideboard into my mouth, being propelled sheerly by my "will" to have it.
xxxxxxxxxxxxxxxxxxxxxxxxxxxxxxxxxxxxxxxxxxxxxxxxxxx
x

*

101 Burdett Road,
Bow, E.3.
Tues. Feb 29. 1944

My Darling,
The all-clear has just gone after a very dull alert, and very soon I hope to be tucked up warmly in bed for the rest of the night. (?)

I think mother has gone to bed wearing everything (including her battle-bloomers) except her hat and shoes.

Well, dearest, I started off well this week. I worked until 7.0p.m. on Monday, and was well tucked into my job at 6.15p.m. when the boss came in and put a slip into my hand as he passed my board. It was my rise of 10/-. I finished what I was doing, and them went to his office to say "Thanks for the rise", and to tell him I had applied for my Grad I.E.E.. He said – to put it into his own words "Its quite O.K. about the rise, you are doing all right here, and there will be more rises to follow". So I am now looking forward to another 10/- rise in another three months. I can smell which way the wind is blowing, and I may even get a more responsible job and a £1 rise.

Well, darling, my full wages are now £6-10-6d per 48hr. week, which ain't so bad if you say it quickly and forget that income tax takes £2-6-6d. In fact, people can even get married on it.

Time is getting on now, sweetheart, so I really must close,
I love you, darling,
Cheerio,
Len
xxxxxxxxxxxxxxxxxxxxxxxxxxxxxxxxxxxxxxxxxxxxxxxxxxxx
x

*

101 Burdett Road,
Bow. E.3.
Wed. 8 March, 1944.

My darling,
First, dearest, I must express to you my very deepest apologies for not writing yesterday, but something seems to have gone wrong with all the dates this week. Last night, I thought "tomorrows' Tuesday and I'll have to write to my sweetheart", and it was'nt until a few minutes ago, when I dated this letter that I realised today is Wednesday and not Tuesday. I'm terribly sorry, darling, if I have caused you any anxiety, and will try and make up for it with some extra love and kisses over the week-end.

I safely received one dinner ticket, for which I am truly grateful. I am now swotting up my Hebrew, so that I can be an interesting talking-companion to my fellow diner. Mother and I expect to see you over here as usual on Saturday, and one of you can put me to bed when I arrive home in an intoxicated condition early Sunday morning.

Well, my sweetheart, the alert, the alert has gone, nothing has happened, and the all clear has gone, so we are now where we started (expecting another alert). Once again, MRS.DOYLE has gone to bed PREPARED FOR ACTION and ANY EMERGENCY. And what, may the reader enquire, is it that makes MRS.DOYLE feel so CONFIDENT? Aha!! It is BERTRAMS BROWN BATTLE BLOOMERS at 4/6d per pair and only 2 coupons!

Passing from the ridiculous, my darling, I am looking forward to seeing you, holding you, tickling you and squeezing you on Sunday, (They sound like edieval Tortures, don't they?), So chin-chin for now, dearest,
All my love,
Len.
P.S. – If you are on speaking terms with Eddie, please tell him I may call round about 6.0p.m on Sat.
Xxxxxxxxxxxxxxxxxxxxxxxxxxxxxxxxxxxxxxxxxxxxxxxxxxxx
x

*

Tues. 14 March, 1944.

My Darling Lily,
      Well, its tuesday to-day (I hope), and I have carefully checked up the date. My diary says its tuesday, The "Daily Telegraph" says its tuesday and so does the "Evening News" and mid-day "Standard". The calendar at work says "tuesday", mother says its "tuesday" and father says its "tuesday" and father says its "tuesday".
      So it must be tuesday . So what? So I ups an' I sez, !If its tuesday then I must write ti me future better arf." So I gets out me pen and paper an I writes, an' wat I writes is wat follows, an' as I writes I thinks, "If to-days tuesday, then tomorrow must be Wednesday, an' though I've sed its tuesday on this 'ere letter, wen me sweetie gits it, it will be wednesday, an' she might think its tuesday 'cos I sez so wen I begins.
      Now aint that queer? An'it quite got me all worried, 'cos I don't wants to go putting no calenders back, if yer gits wot I means. So I ups an' I thinks "If I goes on a-talkin' like this, then me darlin' 'll think Im all uneddicated, so I better starts spouting like the nobs and people called Basil oughter spout". So 'ere goes from now on:-
      Well, dearest, there is'nt a great deal of news. I have been released from my fire-guard duty Wednesday evening, so that I may go to my I.E.E. meeting.
      The wardens came round on Monday to try out the stirrup pump and see if it was in good working order, but father would'nt let them touch it – all he did was to tell them the politicians let us down after the last war, and that Herbert Morrison should not be in the cabinet – although what all this has got to do with inspecting a stirrup pump, I really don't know. Anyhow the result was that I tried the damn thing out tonight, and it works O.K.
      This, of course, started mother off, who now wants all the gas-masks tested, but I quietened her down by saying that five and a half ton bombs were far more deadly than gas, and she has now vowed that she wont undress again until the war is over.
      I wrote Eddie (Mr. Glover to you, darling) a short letter on Monday, telling him it was O.K. for Sunday. If I'm

not careful, I'll be back into the subject of tuesday again, and I think we've had enough of that for one letter.

The wireless has just stopped dead (10.10pm), and mother is now rushing around preparing for action. Aha! Britains secret weapon is in place, and all preparations have now been made (except unlocking of shelter) to withstand the enemys onslaught.

Time is now 10.20pm, and mother is feverishly searching the heavens for signs of enemy activity. She has left the front room door open, and its _____ cold.

The discovery has now been made that father has the shop key with him, and at this very moment (10.25pm) he is being very much praised (?) by mother. Will the whoosher never go?

Mother is now sitting in the armchair knit, _____ knit, knit, knit _____ aha! Dropped a stitch _____ or was it a gun? No! a stitch _____ knit, knit, knit _____.

Well, my dearest, I have really been in the mood for writing tonight, and, although, perhaps, this has not been a passionate love-letter, I do sincerely hope it has interested and entertained you. I love you, darling, and am looking forward to the week end. Time is now 10.33 and still no siren; yards & yards of knitting are flowing from mothers needles.

Hark! Hark! The Lark? No! (10.35p.m). There will now be an interval of 10 mins.

Well, sweetheart, the warning has gone, mother is safely in the shelter, the oil stove lit, and father on guard at the back door.

There has just been an interval of 40 mins while I have been downstairs because of the gentleman upstairs, but it is all quiet again. There are fires in a N.S.E.W. direction, as they say on the radio. I am thinking about you on fireguard, darling.

The "all clear" is just going, so I will now have to close.

God bless you, and keep you safe, my sweetheart,
All my love,
Len.

xxxxxxxxxxxxxxxxxxxxxxxxxxxxxxxxxxxxxxxxxxxxxxxxxxx
x   *

101 Burdett Road,
Bow. E.3.
Tues. 21/3/44

My darling,
    Once again I pick up my pen (after filling it with ink), and seat myself at the table, to send to you, my sweetheart, the news of the past few (two, to be precise) days.

The builders occupied the kitchen at 8.0a.m. today, and the kitchen is in a proper _____ mess, i.e. it looks like a dogs dinner mixed with the cats breakfast all gone wrong. The crockery, bread bin and variouse other items of like nature have been evacuated to the front room. On my left is the cheese grater, cocoa whisk, Bourn – Vita, Sanatogen and Stomach Power.

To my right, in a slightly North-Easterly direction is the ration book holder, tea cosy, tea pot and curling tongs.

Immediately in front of my writing pad is on cake tin (empty), the scissors, three bottles of medicine and one comb. On the mantlepiece behind me there is a carton of corn paste, comb and brush.

In the centre of all this old junk is – (ME), aspirating for inspiration, which will not come 'cos I have been working very hard and feel very tired.

There isnt really very much more to say, dearest, except "I love you, darling", and with those words I really must close, or I will soon be asleep.
                Cheerio, chin-chin
         Tra –la-la-la, etc....,
              All my love,
                Len.
xxxxxxxxxxxxxxxxxxxxxxxxxxxxxxxxxxxxxxxxxxxxxxxxxxx
x

*

101 Burdett Road,
Bow. E.3.
Tuesd. 28 March '44

My dearest,
          Here is your usual letter with Leonard Doyle scribing it.
          I expect the first thing you want to know is if there is any news from Barking. Well, there aint, and I aint got no proper shut-eye since last Sunday.
          I am talking to Harry on Friday the books we were talking about on Sunday; it will be an excuse to go over there, and I can give them some more encouragement to go.
          I hope you soberly (I think that's the word) realise, darling, that our troubles might not end with Edna and Harry moving. The landlord can raise the rent if he so wishes; also he might want to give other people on his waiting list priority.
          Barking Council may also have a say in the matter, and state that houses are reserved for people with children. Even so, I would sink to any depths of low cunning to get the place.
          Well, sweetheart, I added up my savings last night. They come to 121694 farthings, including income-tax Past-War Credit, four 2 1/2d stamps, one 1d stamp and two empty beer-bottles. Now work out how much I have saved, and if you get it (isn't this scratching out terrible?) right, I will give you an extra kiss on Sunday.
          I love you, darling,
               Ta-ta till Sunday,
                    All my love,
                         Len, xxxxxx
P.S. – all the following is where I tried to fold letter to about ¼ " square, and hide it in the envelope, but it would'nt work.

(Nanna worked out the financial answer on the envelope!)

*

                              101 Burdett Road,
                                      Bow. E.3.
                                      Tues. 4444

My dearest,
          Its Tuesday again, and no exceptional news for you, so I really don't know what to ~~wright right~~ (oh, curse this language!) write (that's right) about.
          I have just been round the docks with my mum, on a 56 bus. Coo, its put the wind up 'er proper. Anyone would think WE were going to be invaded.
          I am going to clean our cycles up on Friday, and we are going for miles and miles on Sunday. I hope it's a nice day, as I'm looking forward to getting a break in the country.
          Well, darling, I've got a lot of notes, etc., to write, so will soon have to close. I am hoping to see you about 10a.m. on next Saturday.
                    Cheerio, my sweetheart,
                    All my love
                                   Len
xxxxxxxxxxxxxxxxxxxxxxxxxxxxxxxxxxxxxxxxxxxxxxxxxxx
x

B.L.DOYLE. Grad I.E.E
          Looks all right, doesn't it?

P.S. – We are getting paid on Wednesday this week instead of Friday, its something to do with Pay as you Earn.

                              *

>101 Burdett Road,
>Bow. E.3.
>Tues. 11/4/44

My darling Lily,
         Heres me calling you again. I hope you are enjoying work after the Easter break. It was very dull on fireguard yesterday, but I did'nt do so bad, 'cos I sneaked out and saw "Snow White and the Seven Dwarfs" in the afternoon, and had tea in the cinema café. It cost me 5/- altogether, but I'm claiming that back as expenses.
         So my darling, who was going to get up early enough to walk to the station with me, didn't leave for home until after 11.0a.m. and to think I was expecting her to bring me in a cup of tea at 6.0a.m! Tut – tut, I really am surprised.
         The effects of the cycle ride have now worn off, and I'm all set for next Saturday. If it is of any interest to you, my exams finish the week end before Whitsun, and I'm on fireguard all day Whit-Saturday.
         Well, dearest, so I will now sign off. Please remember me to Eddie & all the girls.
         Ta-ta, chin-chin. & cheerio,
              All my love,
                  Len
xxxxxxxxxxxxxxxxxxxxxxxxxxxxxxxxxxxxxxxxxxxxxxxxxxxxx

*

101 Burdett Road,
Bow. E.3.
Tues. 18/4/44

My darling sweetheart,

You old whisky-drinker! My mun told me all about it – how you first giggled & then hiccuped and finally walked (?!!*?!) home to the three brass balls. I wonder that you were sober enough to get up and go to work in the morning. Anyhow, you beat dad to it, so I suppose that's something in your favour. Mother has just said you again forgot to take the paper with you on Monday.

Well, dearest, I have already filled half a page up and I hope you don't take it too seriously – I don't really mean it, sweetheart, and think you're a darling. (even if you do go out whisky-drinking.)

I left work at 4.0p.m. today to go to a discussion at the institute. (Mother has just said she did'nt only have dad boozed, she had Lily boozed, too, on Sunday night.)

To continue; it was lovely out this afternoon; I came out of the institute about 7.15pm and had a walk round Trafalgar Square & then came home. (Mother has just said I should'nt write things like that in my letter, you might think I mean it).

Well, my darling, it was'nt so bad at Plesseys on Sunday. Four of us "brains" (me and three others) sat up talking about atheism, the church, the Salvation-army, and such other money-making rackets, until 12.30p.m. By which time we had had half a dozen boots chucked at us, and learnt many new swear-words from people who wanted to sleep. Someone had smuggled some cocoa in, so we all had half a pint (of cocoa) & then went to sleep.

I am going to have a try at converting you over the week-end.

Well, dearest darling, I think that's about all for now,
All my love,
Len

xxxxxxxxxxxxxxxxxxxxxxxxxxxxxxxxxxxxxxxxxxxxxxxxxxx
xxxxxxxxxxxxxxxxxxxxxxxxxxxxxx

(picture of bottle!)

P.S. – The kisses are for you, not for the bottle (which had milk in it)

*

101 Burdett Road,
Bow. E.3.
Tues. April 25. 1944

My darling BXJR/487/3,

Here I am again after another hectic days work. With sweat pouring from my brow I am trying desperately to think of something to say – I went to Barking to collect mother last night, but that was only routine stuff.

I hope you were'nt too late on Monday.

This afternoon at work a 'phone call came throu' to the office – "Will Mr. Doyle & Armstrong please call in at A.R.P. control room as soon as possible". We both went down there, and were chewed up for excessively charging travel expenses for Easter Monday fireguard period. Whereupon I pointed out that the law states every person is to receive a holiday on the bank holiday days, and Easter Monday was bank holiday; hence we were entitled to one day in lieu of, with pay.

Upon which the gentleman interviewing us said there was still no reason for claiming 12s/6d for a 1s/2d trolleybus ride. I nearly told him that the super and tea cost me 6/-, but thought I'd better not. Anyhow, we got away with It & did not have to refund any of the money.

So father and I can now go to drink together.

Well, my sweetheart dearest, there is nowt more to say. Please remember me to Eddie,
All my love, darling,
Cheerio,

AVH2/190/3

xxxxxxxxxxxxxxxxxxxxxxxxxxxxxxxxxxxxxxxxxxxxx

xxx

Please remember me to all the BXJR's/487's.

X

*

101 Burdett Road,
Bow. E.3.
Tues. 2/5/44

My dearest,
      Here, once again, am I writing to you, my darling, although there is practically no news for you.

      I hope you safely arrived at work on Monday, gave Eddie his folder and collected cash (+ 10% holiday bonus) for same. I will be very much obliged if you would ask him to make enquiries in the office at W.T.C. and see if they have my Higher Nat. Certificate, as I have not yet received the actual certificate, and its high time I did 'cos I sat for the exam nearly a year ago now.

      Well, dearest, I really am hard at it this week, trying to learn sumfink, in spite of the lovely weather. How are your bones after Sunday? The lilac (?) you brought over still looks bright and glorious. Need I mention that the beer was finished up on Monday by my mum? Well, sweetheart, I'm afraid, that's all for now, am looking forward to seeing you as bright & fresh on Saturday as you were on Sunday,

      All my love, darling.
          Chin-chin,
            Len
   xxxxxxxxxxxxxxxxxxxxxxxxxxxxxxxxxxxxxxxxxxx
xxx

*

101 Burdett Road,
Bow. E.3.
Wed, May 10, '44.

My darling Lily,
          It's now Wednesday (the day after Tuesday) and I have just read through your letter of the 9th inst.

    Well, sweetheart, I hope you enjoyed Eileen Harrods visit – she is'nt a bad girl, really, 'though she does talk rather a lot – you might give her my best wishes & kind regards next time you see her.

    You say in your letter you should'nt have heard yourself think: come to that, Ive never heard you think, either. What conclusions am I to draw? Talking about draws, I asked the typist if she kept carbons in her draws, and she has'nt spoken to me since.

    I am glad you have got your suit for THE DAY, although darling, I always like you in a bright frock or skirt & blouse, best.

    How short is the skirt going to be? (!!!*#)

    Thank you for your thoughts about me on Sunday morning, my darling. My cold (which I never had) is now quite better.

    Although I would like to see the "Song of Russia!", I think you had better go as I may have too much swotting to do.

    I expect the music by chickoskey (I hope thats spelt rightly) will be a bit of all right.

    It WAS NOT the doctor who committed all the murders in "Ten Little Niggers", but my price for saying who it was is 10gs.

    Cheerio for now, darling
    Looking forward to Sunday,
    Len
xxxxxxxxxxxxxxxxxxxxxxxxxxxxxxxxxxxxxxxxxxxx
xxx

*

101 Burdett Road,
Bow. E.3.
16 May 1944.

My dearest darling,
I am afraid your letter is going to be very short this week, sweetheart, as I am extremely busy. Also, my sweet, your letter has taken second precedence to a letter to a soldier – Fred Venour. We received another air mail from him today, and I simply had to reply. I promised him a nice long letter in another eight days, and I'm afraid this will have to apply to you, to, darling,
So All my love,
Len
xxxxxxxxx
xxxxxxxxx
xxxxxxxxx
P.S. – Because I've sent you a short letter, does'nt mean yours to me has got to be short, too.

*

101 Burdett Road,
Bow. E.3.
Wed. 24-5-44.

My dearest darling,
I have just filled my pen with ink, got sheets of blotting paper and quires of writing paper, and am all set for my letter to you, sweetheart. All the material is ready, and I am now collecting my thoughts and beginning to concentrate. Aha! I remember! I have just returned from a bike ride to Barking to collect THAT HAT of Ednas for mother. I left here at 6.45p.m and was back again by 8.15pm, with the hat safely in the saddle-bag. It's a pity the hat & saddle bag are not the same shape, although by the time I got home with the hat, both hat & bag were near enough the same shape; and after all that, mother has decided she does'nt like the hat, after all. So now I suppose I'll have to take it back.

Well, darling, I am glad to see you arrived at work early on Monday, but you had better not do that too often, or they'll think you're crazy.

Everything went smoothly on Tuesday night, although I don't think I got a distinction. Bill turned up for the exam, and when we were all going into the pub afterwards, he refused to come, 'cos hes a communist, atheist and teetotal. As I was his pal and shared the same views, I didn't go either. So we both walked all the way home with a 15minute interval in the park for a smoke.

When we got to my back door, under the T.B.B. (three golden spheres), I asked him to come in and have a pint of cocoa, an' he said "right Len, I don't mind if I do", so we goes up the stairs and opens the door, an' guess what? There was ma with only her nightdress on, doing her hair! When she saw Bill, she bolted up the passage like a rabbit into its burrow. I've never seen a woman run so fast from a man.

Well, darling, after I had brought Bill round, out comes ma with her dressing gown on, and settled once again to do her hair.

Talking about bringing someone round, dad said have you any gin, please?

Regarding your letter of last week, dearest, I am very pleased to see you have made the pillows for me to rest my head on. May I suggest that, under the circumstances, two heads are better than one?

Commenting on Eddies loose leaf builders, I am pleased to see he has intentions, at least, of still carrying on next term. Please don't get the words "carrying on" misinterpreted.

You might tell him that, on the whole, Hackney is a lot easier than Willesden – almost on the same scale as Poplar, in fact.

I love you darling, and you are as soft & lovely and as kissable this week-end as you were last.

I would very much like to go biking some time over Whitsun, but if you don't feel A.1., will not press the point.

I love you, darling (or have I said that before?)

All is O.K. for Sunday – 11.0a.m. Aldgate East Ticket Hall, and don't forget the gin – and I really will have to close now, as I am not quite in the mood for letter-writing, and my thoughts are not flowing as smoothly and naturally as I like them to when writing a long letter. So this is the end, as the puppy said when his tail was docked,

    Cheerio my sweetheart,
    All my love,
      Len

P.S. – Don't forget the darling gin – I mean gin, darling.

xxxxxxxxxxxxxxxxxxxxxxxxxxxxxxxxxxxxxxxxxxxxxxxxxxxxx
x

*

101 Burdett Road,
Bow. E.3.
Wed. 7 June 1944

My darling sweetheart,
                    Your letter to me, and mother's birthday gift arrived at the same time, and mother wishes me to thank you very much for the stockings.

    Yes, my dear, the balloon certainly does seem to have gone well and truly up. Mother said she wept when she saw all the soldiers going up the road in full war kit on Monday; and for the first time in ten years I prayed for the wind to drop on tuesday evening.

    Bill (the one you've heard of, but never seen) came up on tuesday evening, and brought some records with him. They were all classicals, but were very "go-ey", and I certainly like his taste in music. He had the whole of "The Sorcerer's Apprentice", on (I think), three records, and it sounded jolly good. I'll have to introduce you to Bill one day – he's a very bright silly ass, if you know what I mean. We stayed up to hear the midnight news, and I did'nt get to bed until 1a.m.

    Well, darling, tonight, I have just been to the pictures & seen "Andy Hardys Blonde trouble". It was funny all the way through.

    Thank you very much, dearest, for your kind words re my classes. A complement like that goes a long way to warming my heart (or should I say to giving me a swelled head?)

    I am glad to see you are doing your bit for the Red Cross & St. Johns, but I wish you got a percentage of the rake-off.

    So a spider is'nt an insect after all. Did you spot this weeks deliberate mistake? How can a <u>mandrake</u> (or may drake) be a duck? Anyhow, you pluck it and see (I thought that was rather crude).

    We had the radio on all day at work on Monday, and were continually telephoning the latest news of the invasion all day. My thoughts hav'nt flowed very freely tonight, I'm afraid, so I will now close down. Am looking forward to

seeing you on Saturday (I have to be on fireguard at 3p.m. on Sunday, by the way dear), so take care of yourself,
    All my love,
                                  Len
xxxxxxxxxxxxxxxxxxxxxxxxxxxxxxxxxxxxxxxxxxxxxxxxxxxx

*

101 Burdett Road,
Bow. E.3.
Wed. 21-6-44

My darling Lily,
We is a-getting' on orlrite wir there 'ere flyin' bombs. According to all the district, we 'ad an orful nite last nite, but me, me mumer and farfer did'nt wake up till about five a.m., when we 'erd about six come down in an 'ower. You can tell Eddie the injineering scool as bin damiged again. Well, my sweet, that's the first part of your letter answered.

I am going to lodge a complaint with Herbert Morrison about fireguards being in bed when they should be on duty.

Yours truly has also seen a flying bomb – it was this afternoon, when one was exploded in the air about three miles from where I work. I am very pleased, my darling, that you have managed to get the tickets for Lupino Lane. I have just told mother I am going, and there will now be a 30 minute interval while I bring her round. So another Lord is a man after all? Well, well, I am surprised. Its marvellous the things thay can do nowadays.

Bill (I believe you've heard of him) and myself went to a Public Lecture on "Electronics for the layman" at West Ham Municiple college on tuesday evening. It was entirely free and open to the Public, and most of the people there were young chaps, like ourselves, with a sprinkling of older men and one young lady.

Anyhow, what I am coming to is that there was one old girl there (she must have been about 70), and who looked – and was dressed like – a regular old churchgoer. She must have got to the lecture by mistake, and me and Bill reckon she thought electronics was something immoral, and was there to represent the church and keep it in order.

My Jewish friend at work has now put out enquiries re flats, and is still very optimistic. He said we could easily buy a house, anyhow.

I expect we could if we had the money. I am calling in at Gibbons on Saturday (flying bombs, etc. permitting), to enquire about furniture coupons, etc.

I now feel a lot better, and am proceeding satisfactoraly.

Regarding sweet rations, sweetheart, I advise you to eat at least 4ozs of yours right now, 'cos I've ate 4ozs. of mine.

My mum said she would like 10ounces of pale blue knitting, yarn, please.

I am posting my application re evening class instructor, with this letter, but must admit I feel a bit scared because the bloke who reads it is a Doctor of Physics (Ph.D.), Master of Science (M.Sc.), associate member of the Institute of Civil Engineers (A. M. Inst. C. E.), and associate member of the institute of mechanical Engineers (A. M. I. mech. E.). Anyhow, I've hoped for the best and put "Graduate I.E.E" after my name.

Well, my darling, I have rather a lot to do – beds to make, a technical book to read, and a murder story to finish, so I will now close.

Cheerio for now,
All my love,
Len
xxxxxxxxxxxxxxxxxxxxxxxxxxxxxxxxxxxxxxxxxxxxxxxxxxx

This was posted on thursday morning, to let you know we'er all O.K.

*

101 Burdett Rd.,
Bow E.3.
Mon. 26/6/44

My dearest Lily,
    I expect you will be rather surprised to receive this short note, and you may not be pleased to hear that, owing to these flying bombs, I don't think we will be able to visit Horsham this week-end.

    Half the windows in our office were blown out on Sunday night, and the other half this afternoon when the bomb fell nearby.

    Anyhow, darling, I would very much like to meet you on Wednesday, if you can manage it. Shall we say, 6.30p.m. at charing cross? If you like to 'phone tomorrow (Tuesday) at 9.0.p.m., I shall be listening, darling,
        Cheerio for now,
          All my love,
                Len
xxxxxxxxxxxxxxxxxxxxxxxxxxxxxxxxxxxxxxxxxxxxxxxxxxx
x

P.S. – I realise you might be doing overtime on tuesday, so if you don't phone, or can't get thro', I shall be waiting for you at Charing Cross on Wed. (I love you, darling).

*

> 101 Burdett Rd,
> Bow.E.3.
> 11/7/44.

My dearest Lily,

Only a couple of lines to draw your attention to the enclosed. I have just finished writing letters, etc., am very tired & am now going to bed.

Please remember me to Eddie, my darling,

Cheerio,

All my love,

Len

*

                              101 Burdett Rd.,
                                   Bow. E.3.
                              Thurs. 10-8-44.

My dearest darling sweetheart,
         Well, I have just returned from Horsham after Harrys funeral, and all went off smoothly.
         A man from Harrys firm came down at 3.30p.m. with two wreaths from the firm. He was in tears, and said that Edna would hear further.
         Aunty Mabel was also there, and Mr. & Mrs. Philpotts visited the grave just as we left the cemetry.
         Well, darling, so much for that; I will tell you more about it on Saturday.
         The more I think of living at Edna's, the less I like the idea. Anyhow, darling, the local papers will be out tomorrow, and I will write off immediately if I see anything suitable.
         Thats all for now, sweetheart; I am looking for Saturday,
                    Au revoir, & all my love,
                              Len.
xxxxxxxxxxxxxxxxxxxxxxxxxxxxxxxxxxxxxxxxxxxxxxxxxxxx
x

                              *

(envelope marked <u>URGENT</u>)
(Post Mark - 16th August 1944)

101 Burdett Rd.,
Bow. E.3.
Tues.

My darling Lily,

    A few lines to tell you that a most important thing has been omitted – you forgot to sign the Banns of St.Luke.

    I am therefore coming over straight from work tonight (Wednesday) and will bring the wretched thing with me. I will only be able to stay a few minutes, as I must get straight home to get them to the Vicarage, and then go on to Ednas.

Cheerio, ducks.
Len.

*

1949

                                        101 Burdett Road
                                        Bow. E.3.
                                        27. May 1949

My Darling wife,
    The time is 10.30p.m., and I have just
returned from the 'Brit' after celebrating in the traditional
fashion our lovely event.
  I have been thinking absolutely of you and our son
ever since I left you both, my dearest sweetheart, and never
did I believe that I could have such mixed emotions – supreme
joy and happiness at seeing our dear son, and sorrow that my
own dear heart had to bear such pain and anxiety to give him
that life which is so precious to both of us.
  I love you, my darling; but never through our joyful
marriage has it been so brought home to me just how close
and near you are to me; never – until this moment – have I
considered how dreadfully empty and useless my life would
have been had you not survived your ordeal, my faithful
lovely wife. To think on this now has utterly made me realise
that we are, indeed united, and to lose you or our darling son
would be like losing part of my own body.
  Now that I have been able to express – quite
inadequately, I am afraid – my true and sincere feelings to my
darling wife and – oh! – so precious – son, you will realise just
how important it is for you to make a complete recovery, to
rest all you can and not to do anything that you do not quite
feel up to – not even letter writing, knitting or reading.
  Although I originally wished for a girl (and who
wouldn't after being married to its darling mother for four
years) – I already love my son – yes, MY son, darling – as
much as I love his dear mother.
  And that's a heck of a lot.
  So you see, dearest, I love you. I always will love
you, and never will you find wanting the reliance that you
place in me in times such as this.
  When I first saw Michael I didn't know whether to
laugh or cry, he looked so cute, and I now humbly replace my
statement that all babies are ugly with the remark that all
babies except ours are ugly.

And ugly or not I love him.
My mum and dad and all your family want me to tell you this, that & t'other, but as this letter is straight from my heart to your heart, dearest, I will leave such mundane things until I see you this evening.
   That's all for now; all my deepest, sincerest, love and affection my sweetheart,

     Your ever-loving & faithful husband,

         Len

P.S. – Give my love to Michael next time you feed him, and tell him daddy is strengthening his cot to make sure it will take all of his seven lbs ten.

       *

Printed in Great Britain
by Amazon